EVERYTHING'S GOING TO BE OKAY

How to Nurture Yourself During a Storm

CHAVA FLORYN

Illustrations copyright © 2022 by Chava Floryn
Artwork by Yehudis Tombosky
Cover Design by JL Woodson

ISBN 978-1-0880-9872-1 (hardcover)
First Edition: September 2022

Twin Rose Media Publishing
chavatombosky@gmail.com

For Robbie, my love

TABLE OF CONTENTS

PART 1

FACING THE UNCERTAINTY

There is a stained-glass window in my kitchen that catches the light of the first rays of sun each morning. Round, jewel-toned glass panels scatter a kaleidoscope of patterns, the colors singing of the art-deco past, while simultaneously capturing my present.

My eyes glide down to the bottom corner of one windowpane, where I catch a glimpse of a fracture. Sharp edges are suspended in crystal; the bones are there but the soul is gone. As the light catches the sharper fractals, a stronger warmth bathes my body. The resolute broken fractals hang on, clutching the sill like prey on a web begging to stay whole. Like the disruption that sets in during a crisis, it's no longer perfect, but it has its own structure now. Isn't that the brutality of chaos? The imperfect ruffling of our lives and the determined reset that comes after.

CHAPTER 1

EGBOK

"EGBOK," I said—half believing it, half acting—as I leaned over and kissed my husband's feverish forehead. Eighteen months after the pandemic started, on the day of my niece's wedding—which my husband, the rabbi, was to officiate, as I was about to get dressed into my beautiful green gown, I felt my husband's body and he was burning up. Then came the vomiting and coughing. I called a medic from our Las Vegas hotel to check his vitals. Robbie's temperature was one hundred and five degrees.

This was no average illness. Twenty-six years of being married to this man had taught me that Robbie would never miss his niece's wedding. He could weather anything with a few Tylenol and a smile. No, this was different. He tried to get out of bed three times, even forcing himself down the stairs and across the gargantuan casino to print the marriage contract. A feat that left him weaker than ever. "Go to the wedding," he begged me. "I'll be fine," he said. But there are moments in your life when you see something no one else sees, not even the patient himself, and you lean into that instinct with all of your damn self.

Instead of attending a wedding, I put Robbie in a wheelchair and we rushed off to the worst place in a mid-COVID world: an ER off the Las Vegas strip. It felt like wandering into a shelter on Skid Row, slipping on vomit, only to be told, "We are short staffed and have no more beds…or paper-towels. Wait here and try not to die."

Dr. G, the head ER doctor, confirmed my husband's illness was grave. His organs were failing due to a life-threatening septic infection. "We are packed tonight but I will get you into the system as quickly as I can," he said. Robbie had less than forty-eight hours before falling into irreversible septic shock. We were hitting our twenty-ninth hour since Robbie's first sign of fever.

There were ten patients to one nurse. Robbie was put in a reclining chair, which he sat in with a climbing fever for twenty-one hours, until we finally left the decrepit ER and made it to the cardiac floor. If this was the Las Vegas ticket to hell, we had clearly landed in sin city. From my own experience, saying "EGBOK" (which stands for "Everything's Going to Be Okay") did not always mean things turned out optimally. If there's anything the pandemic has taught us, it's that sometimes things don't turn out okay.

I felt like my world was raining shrapnel. If the worst outcome came to pass, and I was left a widow on a mid-pandemic vacation, how would any of this really be okay? 'EGBOK' felt like the end of a pollyannaish balloon string I grabbed to keep me grounded. I've weathered crisis before. But this particular crisis felt different. Because now I was asked to take that leap of faith drinking a piña colada at the Palazzo after pacing in my husband's hospital room inhaling disinfectant all day. This crisis felt different because this was the love of my life suffering, and the impact of losing him would massively shift the trajectory of my life forever. Also we were on a family vacation! One day earlier we were taking family photographs.

I had planned that perfect photo shoot for weeks. My middle daughter was finally home from college for summer break. Our youngest son was about to head out to college for his first year along with our daughter overseas. I wanted that last picture before everyone went their separate ways come fall—before the final empty nesting. We had just chosen the picture that would grace our living room mantel. It would replace the last photo we had there, taken eleven years prior. Just the day before Robbie fell ill, we were wandering through the streets with our photographer, seizing the day. Capturing the moment of our children on the cusp of adulthood, our love ready to morph into those "golden years" where less responsibility and more playfulness was promised.

And now this fresh hell. *Everything's going to be okay?* More like, everything was going to shit.

Yet I declared "EGBOK" anyway when the doctor said my fifty-year-old husband would need to be admitted into the hospital with confirmed sepsis as a result of either leukemia or a heart attack—possibly both.

CHAPTER 2

IS EVERYTHING GOING TO BE OKAY?

"EGBOK," my sister Mimi, then only twenty years old, said as she squeezed my hand while on an airplane to Chico, California. She desperately tried to catch my eye, searching for affirmation. She wanted me to say that I believed we were about to enter our father's hospital room to say hello rather than goodbye. My eyes avoided hers. I knew I could not give her that promise.

Growing up, my dad used the Disney-esque mantra when we were faced with situations we knew we couldn't change. "EGBOK," he'd say with a twinkle in his eye, like he was Jiminy Cricket willing magic into existence.

My dad was an optimist, but first and foremost he was a scientist and a realist. He was a physician who healed many patients; he also buried the ones he couldn't cure. He lost his own father at the tender age of nine. He knew as well as anyone that things did not always turn out okay. So why did he tell us they would? What was the real purpose for him saying "EGBOK" in the face of uncertainty?

My six siblings and I entered the hospital holding our breath. It was July 2010. I can still feel the hot summer air bracing our tormented bodies. When we arrived at Enloe hospital in Chico California, three nurses, with tears brimming, were standing outside looking at us, all of them knowing who we were and what we were about to walk into. They had never met us before, but they knew. My father was the head gastroenterologist at the same hospital that now held his body in an ICU on life support. His story left everyone who worked with him shaken, disbelieving. Like a slow motion scene, our feet took up a rhythm against the tile of the hospital hallway. Like the halls my father walked through while he practiced medicine for over thirty years. I counted my steps. One, two, three, four…how many steps would it take to arrive at his doorstep, to learn the truth? How many steps for our world to change? Each sound of our soles held a cacophony of angst against the silence we would endure minutes later when he took his last breath.

According to eyewitness accounts, my father's second wife of only four short years, had brought him into the hospital unconscious. To my knowledge, they had been separated for about a year and a half. My father, my aunt, and several of my father's colleagues told us it was the first time she had ever formally visited Chico since their separation. None of us had really gotten to know her. I had only met her once. She wore sunglasses during our entire visit. Upon learning he was brain dead, three days after dropping my dad off at the hospital, the nurses reported she left town without telling any of us that he was breathing through a ventilator, barely conscious.

We found out he was in the ICU four days after his arrival by accident. A sheriff greeted us with questions about the circumstances surrounding my father's demise. Both the nursing staff and the sheriff were suspicious, but no one was ever brought in for formal questioning. Because of the suspicious circumstances, the state refused to release my father's body without performing an autopsy. To this day, there has never been any closure to the circumstances surrounding my father's death. My father's wife sued me, all my siblings, my grieving grandmother, and my mother a week after we were able to get my father's body out of the hands of the state for burial. Our fate was sealed, and no matter how I tried to will the story differently, I feared nothing would ever be okay after that July twenty-third."

And yet, while my husband's life hung in the balance eleven years later, I still whispered "EGBOK." I didn't invoke that mantra to change fate. History taught me that I did not possess that kind of power. I said it to relinquish my own ego, as it reminded me to yield to a Higher source. I think my father said everything's going to be okay not as a way to avoid reality, but as a way to allow reality to carry him into the next moment. The complexity of how to lean into a crisis is described best in *Tao Te Ching* translated by Derek Lin,

Yield and remain whole
Bend and remain straight
Be low and become filled
Be worn out and become renewed
Have little and receive
Have much and be confused

It is only when we face the gravest of circumstances—when we imagine we can't possibly move through that pain—that we are forced to relinquish our expectations. That is when we finally yield with grace. And it is this act of yielding which has the power to morph us. Like that shrapnel of crystal that dangled inside my breakfast window, where the window was broken in one place and yet still remained intact everywhere else, so is the battle of life. We can remain alive with purpose and with love and still move through the battlefield with our wounds. We can ache alongside our joy. STILL, if it's a shit show now, THEN IT'S A SHIT SHOW NOW. Let's honor that.

The seemingly impossible moments are the ones that allow us to force our own ego aside and free us to give our soul the oxygen we need to reset. Rabbi DovBer Pinson writes in *Reclaiming the Self*, "When the ego collapses under a distressing experience, its resistance to transcendent power is removed." We may not be able to change the circumstances of our lives, or the rules of this mortal game, but we can surely change how we process our destiny.

Being the eldest daughter to a pretty large family and the mother to three of my own kids, I had to navigate some uncharted territory before I figured out how to remove my own ego and surrender, a lesson by the way, I still continually battle to learn. I was twenty-eight when I went from raising two children to five overnight. My third child was born the same day my then ten-year-old and thirteen-year-old brothers came to live with me and my husband. A couple of years after that, my parents got divorced and my thirteen-year-old sister and my eighteen-year-old sister came to live with us. At one point my husband and I were raising seven kids from two to eighteen years old: our three children and four of my siblings.

I found myself overwhelmed by trying to control every outcome. I wanted to say EGBOK and mean it, but I fought it. My ego was resistant and it caused a lot of extra pain that I wish I had learned to harness better. This is the book that I wish I'd had then. Are there better ways to parent like champions...*even during a crisis*? Can we figure out the best way to make everything okay for us and for our families when the chips are down? How do we lean into uncertainty, nurture our relationships in the eye of a storm, and find our way back to our own voice after we have lost it while weathering a crisis?

I think that making everything okay is a beautiful choice we get to (not *have to,* but *get to*) lean into every minute of every day—and not just when things are okay, but when things are extremely not okay. We have an energy that runs through us which is connected to a higher calling, and when we tap into it, it can truly help us find ways to make our lives a little better. This book highlights a few of those ways, through my own lessons as well as the expert advice I was able to unlock while interviewing my incredible guests on *The Nurture Series* podcast.

You know the old adage, "Put your own oxygen mask on first?" Well, welcome, because we're about to put that oxygen on hard. We're going to unleash our best selves, as we turn into the best possible nurturers to others as well. And if you are in the middle of a crisis, grab a bowl of ice cream and dig in, because this book is definitely for you.

Our mind is a working organism, and sometimes it can control us in ways that do not produce the healthiest outcomes. Believe me, if you lived in my head, it would sometimes be like walking down a dark alley leading to a brick wall (with lots of people pointing and laughing, I might add). This is the reason I read and ask questions of the experts. Because they make me find a way out of the darkness and into my transcendent power.

Without the work I had put into creating this book, I believe I would have had a much more difficult time forging through the unknown during my husband's out-of-the-blue illness. If I said this book—the interviews, and personal work I was fortunate to have with Therapist Joan Rosenberg, Communication Coach Lauren Weinstein, Inner Bonding Expert Dr. Margaret Paul, Health Coach Lock Hughes, Performance Coach Aman Sood, Energy Healer Hanna Gedy, and Social Worker Sharon Roszia—was the exact EGBOK medicine I needed to move through the most uncertain experience of my life to date, it would be an understatement. (There are way more interviews I've conducted with therapists and coaches, some of whom I've had the pleasure to work with personally to date, but those are the ones which I've highlighted in this book.)

This book is here to help you set your own vision for coping like a champion. Even when the chips are down. Maybe especially when the chips are down. My hope is that through my personal stories, and the expert guidance and advice from folks way smarter than me, we will forge through life's darkness better than okay. Saying "EGBOK" won't necessarily change your outcomes, but it will certainly change how you face them. And if you can't say EGBOK today, please don't. Let's go on this journey together.

CHAPTER 3

UNCERTAINTY IS CERTAIN

O ur trip to Las Vegas was meant to be extremely memorable for all three of our children. Obviously we got more than we bargained for. But, as my mom loves to say often, "Man plans and God laughs." God was definitely having some giggles. For a minute there, it felt like God had turned on the Tombosky channel and said, "Let's see what happens when I touch this button. Sepsis. Cool, don't change the station, I love this part."

2021 had already started out pretty challenging as a result of the pandemic. Our daughter had just come back from her year at university in Israel, where all of her classes were held inside her dorm room via Zoom. To top it off, she had just spent the month of June living in a bomb shelter under a barrage of rockets due to the latest Israeli-Palestinian conflict which arose that spring. I was not sleeping very well as a result. However, by June fifteenth everything seemed to brighten. The cease-fire began, our daughter made her way home safely, Covid *seemed* to be a thing of the past. And we were off to celebrate a family milestone: Our youngest son had just graduated high school. Meir had been accepted into college in Israel, and while we would soon have an empty nest, Robbie and I were looking forward to more travel time together, new opportunities and new adventures. We were all finally vaccinated and believed we had made it through the pandemic crisis with flying colors. "We did it!" I thought. "We finally got through it!" We'd weathered lockdowns, lost income, and fear of illness and war. We had lost our family patriarch; I'd sat with my grandfather in his final hours and watched his body decline into the fold of the Universe. The world changed and so did we. It was time to move forward. We were ready for the new excitement life would finally bring us after what felt like a long, eerie silence. We were sure it would be different come the second half of 2021. We were sure a brighter day was up ahead.

So our (fully vaccinated) trip to Las Vegas was a welcome celebration…until it wasn't.

In between coffee breaks in the hospital, a friend and I were in the midst of a DMC (for all those non-millennials out there, a Deep Meaningful Conversation). We were getting into our daily struggles and discussing my new normal when she said, "Everything is so uncertain with this pandemic looming. With Robbie sick, you must be struggling with even more harsh uncertainty, too."

I actually had this crazy revelation in that moment. I responded, "Uncertainty? That is the least of my worries. I haven't had certainty in over ten years. Who lives with certainty?" If my father's sudden death and my husband's out-of-the-blue illness has taught me anything, it's that there's never true certainty. To me, certainty is a rare delicacy, which only a few of us decide to bite into. And with the outbreak of a global pandemic, no one has had that taste for years.

How do we live with uncertainty?

We all react to uncertainty in different ways. The last thing I want anyone to feel when reading this book is that you are not measuring up, not getting it right, or not living productively *enough*. In this moment, you are ENOUGH. You are exactly where you are meant to be. You have more power than you realize and this journey is yours and yours alone to experience. Let's make a deal that we will cherish this time together without the self-criticism.

For example, when the pandemic first hit, I had zero idea how to handle it. Let me tell you a little about my Eat, Pray, Love pandemic journey where I ate all day, prayed I wouldn't get fat, and then loved myself despite the sweatpants that grew around my thicker body like a turtle shell.

I had the indulgent weeks where I consumed artisan bread for daaays, the fit weeks where I was lifting weights almost every day. There were weeks I sat and cried, days when I couldn't get out of bed and Netflixed it for hours, and eventually the period of time I finally got the balance I so needed.

Please don't read this book and feel bad if tomorrow morning, you wake up and say, "Wow, there were such great recommendations to nurture myself and my relationships and to lean into making myself okay during the tough times, but I'm going through a tornado and I'm not in the mood to do any of them. I need a nap." Take that nap. Realize that sleep is going to nurture you back to crushing life again. So yeah, take the nap.

There are no rules when it comes to dealing with uncertainty. There are ways to handle it. There are ways to learn how not to be victimized by it. However, fear cannot be the excuse for losing one's self. That critical, fearful voice is trying to get our attention. It is merely there to be a signal. It is like the defeated soldier who waves his white flag begging for a truce. Fear is there to let your body know there is something you need to deal with. And if you don't listen to the signal, your body will find interesting—and sometimes painful—ways to signal even louder. Disease stands for dis-ease. Something is out of sorts, and the goal is to figure out why that flag is waving. If we allow fear to win then we cannot withstand uncertainty.

The hardest truth we encounter about uncertainty is that uncertainty is certain. Like death and drinking that morning coffee, uncertainty is one of the few things we can count on in life.

And while we might hate it, we can be certain that we're going to be uncertain.

We associate uncertainty with danger. If our brain doesn't know what's around the corner, it will rely on the patterns it has created over time to detect danger, helping us predict what might come next. Psychologists call this ability to predict danger "nexting." Nexting has a way of keeping us safe. It becomes a perpetual pattern in our heads, which can feed on doing the same thing over and over again while expecting a different outcome. Yep, it's nexting which makes us feel insane. Our reptilian brain reacts to the fear of not knowing what is around the corner by going into overdrive. We are incredible at obsessing over the what-if scenarios. Unfortunately, nexting makes us feel like we are under constant attack. What's the worst thing that could happen right now? "UM, EVERYTHING." And that's how the uncertainty creeps in.

One. Bad. Thought. At. A. Time.

My phone rang. "What's wrong with Robbie?" my friend asked, "I saw a group chat praying for him." My mom called: "What's going on—what did the doctors say?" My mother-in-law was frightened and also wanted answers. Our synagogue called: "We're sending food, what's happening now, what should we expect?" It was like a cacophony of questions I was forced to field daily and the only answer I had to give was, "I don't know." I felt a little like a Vegas reporter when I was really born to be a Vegas showgirl.

People demanded certainty and I had nothing to offer but the promise that news would eventually come. The calls felt like a whack-a-mole game that never ended, as did the multiple unanswered questions that I posed to the doctors about Robbie's septic infection. Was it from the vaccine? Did it happen from trying to cut open that coconut with a knife which pierced his hand down to the bone six weeks prior?

And then I noticed the spots.

"Robbie, we should probably tell the doctor about that red dot on your hand."

"Don't bother with that," he said. "It's nothing."

"Yesterday when your fever reached one hundred and five you also said it was nothing. Maybe we should mention the spots," I said.

"Don't mention the spots," he demanded.

So I mentioned the spots.

There are studies that indicate we are capable of being calmer in an anticipated storm than in an unexpected and uncertain outcome. We are more comfortable with definite pain than we are with uncertainty.

If we are told our loved one has an infection, even if that infection is life threatening, if we know the proper diagnosis and how to treat it, we can withstand the moment; we can move into the next situation because there is some familiarity to our fall. Even if our adrenalin goes into overdrive as we run to the nearest safe haven, as we sit in the dark to pray, we can still handle that calmly. But when we sit in the dark with no answers, the lizard brain begins to obsess and freak out because we don't know what to expect— and that is more distressing.

This thought process applies to our health—say, when there's a global pandemic. It applies to our sense of financial safety—like when there are multiple companies closing as a result of the barrage of quarantines, and your job might be at risk. We find these experiences much more distressing than our everyday worries, because we don't know what to expect next. Job uncertainty, for example, takes a larger toll on a person's health than getting fired out of the blue. Like ripping off a Band-Aid; it's less painful to get fired immediately than to wait for months for the impending disclosure that you're out of income. The stress that someone goes through every single day, wondering, "Is tomorrow going to be my last day of work? Will I die in this pandemic? Will my husband make it through this septic infection?" causes us the most harm. Uncertainty is more painful than certainty.

So please take a moment, take a deep breath, and give yourself a pat on the back. You have shown up with courage to tackle this massive mountain called uncertainty. You are here in this moment, and no matter how difficult it has been, you have been fighting like a champion all along. You're still breathing.

During the height of the pandemic, I asked Robbie if he felt I had changed. I wondered if he thought I had become less excited about life. During the quarantine, I had many days where I felt numb, but other days where I felt excited to launch my creative endeavors. And then there were the days I was overwhelmed with fear, boredom, and isolation. Robbie answered me with the most compassionate answer I think we all need to hear in these situations. He said, "You are coping. We are all just coping."

Sustaining discomfort is truly an art, one which I believe we have been blessed to tackle together. For the very first time, the entire world is coping with the same exact uncomfortable event together at the exact same time. Never in the history of the world has there been such a collective consciousness toward managing uncertainty.

We tend to see life as what we think it could become, rather than what it is in this very moment. If we prejudge every experience before it happens, we can fall into the trap of becoming stuck. We no longer learn and grow. We get set in our ways. On the other hand, according to Daeyeol Lee, PhD, a Bloomberg Distinguished Professor of Neuroscience and Psychological and Brain Sciences at Johns Hopkins University, "When you enter a more novel and volatile environment, this might enhance the tendency for the brain to absorb more information." In other words, when you leave your comfort zone, you get stronger and more resilient. You can create new neural pathways and rewire your brain. You have the power to generate new reactions when facing difficult situations.

The Doctor came in and stared at me blankly as I interrupted his daily rotation when I pointed out the spots. "I'm sure it's *nothing*," he responded.

"*Nothing.*" Like the empty promise to care for a dying patient I kept hearing in the emergency room the night before? "We're moving him to the lobby," the nurse said after Robbie and I sat in the ER for eighteen hours while he was on a barely audible IV drip. "We cannot treat this patient any longer as he's officially been admitted and is no longer our responsibility. He'll be *fine.*"

I felt like a caged animal in the middle of a forest fire. "If you do not want the death of my husband on your shoulders, you will absolutely not move us and you will give him his next dose of antibiotics. Otherwise he will not be *FINE.*" I knew that a septic patient has forty-eight hours before they die. I've been a patient advocate for my sister, who deals with a chronic kidney disease, my father, who suffered with heart disease and diabetes, not to mention my grandmothers and my grandfathers. I have often been the first call my family makes when someone is hospitalized.

I checked my watch and counted backward from Robbie's first sign of illness. When we reached the 34th hour without any intervention I knew things were NOT FINE. Time was of the essence and yet my husband only got treatment when I stared the nurse down and begged her to drop protocol and do what was right versus what was hospital policy. My decision to speak up and the nurse's decision to hook Robbie up to an IV antibiotic and not move us to the lobby probably saved his life.

I went to search for my thousandth chocolate pudding when the internist came back barely an hour after I'd mentioned the spots. He actually looked shaken. "The spots, they're not nothing. Does he have them on his feet?" I slipped off Robbie's socks. There, blaring at us, was a much darker red sore on his pinky toe. Apparently that *nothing* was an indication of the source of Robbie's septic infection. The red dots were proof of a heart infection known as endocarditis. After five days, leukemia had finally been ruled out. Robbie needed an angiogram, but his septic infection made that procedure especially risky. After canceling the procedure, it was decided that it was too risky not to have it, and it was scheduled again. "We need to assess this heart infection. He could die on the table. But he could also be fine."

And that's when I went back for another pudding.

Another text broke through. It was my sister: "Do you know when you're coming home," it read. To which I responded, "What happens tomorrow stays in tomorrow, kind of like Vegas."

I did not even know it yet, but this brand of uncertainty was sharpening my neural pathways even better than I already had. I was becoming more resilient.

CHAPTER 4

UNCERTAINTY FROM THE MASTERS

The morning my husband was scheduled for his tenuous heart procedure, my stomach rumbled with caffeine and nerves as I stood inside the Palazzo elevator holding four coffees. One for me, one for each of my kids. I'm not an insane person; I don't buy coffees for children. My kids are grown. My twenty-five-year-old son never experienced profound loss other than losing his grandparents (which I know most kids experience, even though I never experienced losing a grandparent until I was in my early-thirties). Mordy studies existentialism just for fun. He is brilliant and sees the world as a realist with a profound sensitivity to humanity. He wants to understand life so he can process death. He was only ten years old when Robbie's father died, fourteen when my father died. Robbie and I were in our early thirties when we buried our dads. Mordy is probably the one who had to process our pain and loss the most.

Then there's my daughter Yehudis who's twenty-two, beautiful sensitive, and positive to a fault. She has lived through loss. Her best friend, Tsofia, texted her late one night, "I love you," five minutes before she fell out of an automobile that was driving too fast. Tsofia died upon impact. Yehudis was only fifteen when she had to experience the tragedy of burying a best friend. The year before that, Yehudis's other closest friend, Gabby, buried her father, Chris, who was only fifty. He was strong and handsome and healthy every day of his life—until he wasn't. Four months after his fiftieth birthday, he didn't survive a tumor which was wrapped around his dying heart.

My youngest son is Meir. Meir is handsome and bright-eyed and deep, even though he'd rather let you think his good looks indicate a shallow existence. Meir can't remember his dead grandfathers. He has never been to a funeral. I've been excellent at protecting him from mortality. For better or worse, I falsely believed I could keep up that lie for him for a lifetime.

Six in the morning was the part of my day which felt like the commercial break to the crisis, which is why—although I was not a morning person—I got up early. Every day I rode the hotel elevator with our coffees as wistful music and images of hopeful winnings flashed on a screen on the ride to the sixth floor. Elevator music took on new meaning. It was my calm. That elderly couple holding hands? They're just riding the elevator to go somewhere…the next shark exhibit, or the craps table perhaps. Me? I craved that elevator like it was entering an alternate universe. The doors would open and purge me of drunken lost hope and squandered dreams, as the mix of less filtered smokey casino "purified" air flared up my nostrils. While my husband, the rabbi, fought for his life, I swam past spiritual depravity off the strip, gambling on God to sustain my tired bones.

I caught myself in the elevator mirror. To that adorable family (all wearing Hershey T-shirts, pushing their exhausted toddler in the stroller, who can't tell what time it is because of the simulated daylight), I probably looked ready for vacation. My flowing summer dress, my delicately manicured long nails, my brand new balayage blonde flowing hair that I'd ordered from the wig store for the family celebration which had brought us to Nevada must have made me seem like I stepped out of an Instagram vacation reel.

I had been working on myself all year during the quarantine of the century and decided it was time to have my outer appearance reflect the change. I was in ongoing therapy, and had finally faced some difficult truths about my tendencies. I believed I had faced my eleven-year-old grief that began when my father took his last breath. I was stronger, more resilient and hella self-aware. The blonde locks were a welcome and totally new look, which felt fitting. I was new. I was brand spanking new.

I was meditating twice a day. I was listening. Really listening to the sound of my quiet soul. I was working on "becoming super natural" as the Joe Dispenza book indicated. I had purged years of anguish, resentments, and old patterns. My performance Coach, Aman Sood, a monk from Amsterdam, had assured me I had morphed.

"Chava, write down all the ways you find love, joy, peace, enthusiasm, and gratitude." *K, this is going to be easy*, I thought. It wasn't. Joy for me was savoring garlic pasta, connecting with good people, having someone hold me. Those were all external measures I used to experience joy. They were all dependent upon someone or something else. That is how the list went. Every detail of my life had been dependent upon someone else, something else, somewhere else to feed and nourish my existence. I was living an external life, yet wondered why I was so unhappy. I did not even know how to reassess my internal compass. But after months of therapy, energy healing with Hanna Gedy, getting out of my head and into my body, crying on Zoom calls (where I fantasized the monk was selling my confessions to the highest bidder to pay for his mountain excursions, because I was that cynical), I had finally figured out how to go internal. Living internally with joy, gratitude, love—and yes, anger, sadness, judgment and even embarrassment—needed to shift from external gratification to an internal dialogue. I had learned how to morph my creative flow by entering my meditation nature chamber. I learned how to breathe deeper, and stopped having unrealistic expectations of myself. I learned the art of gratitude and began to access joy, inner calm, and peace. My anxiety only came out when my internal needs depended on external outcomes. I did that work. I was over that work. Right?

My husband was fighting for his life in a hospital off the Las Vegas strip and I wondered, would I survive this external outcome that had the potential to impact my world in ways I couldn't even quantify yet? Would I still hear the whispers of my soul ruminating over the noise of the disrupted frequency that lingered daily between the hours I left that hotel elevator music for the hospital? Would those blonde locks staring back at me inside the elevator mirror remind me how far I came or how off the mark I landed?

For the sake of exercising a new muscle, I had to suspend all of my familiar narratives—which were screaming that life was going to hell in a hand-basket. I had to forge through my uncertainty with less fear and more moxie. My hope was that through this particular challenge I would become a better version of myself. I wanted to use this experience to tackle it differently. And while I had the knowledge I needed as my armor to walk into this battle, I also wasn't prepared to have my grief revived, my patterns revisited, or my resentments re-emerge. I realized no matter how "new" I became I would still be doing the work of reframing my reactions for the rest of my life. You don't wake up one day all better. You work on becoming better every day. And that work is a life-long sentence…I mean opportunity. (*See what I did there?*)

We are not the only ones who have lived on this planet with uncertainty. We have over 5,000 years of human behavior to gather data from. Which is why I decided to pull from the most ancient wisdom I know of to get a better understanding of how humans have withstood the challenge of leaning into the fragile unknown.

Let's tackle the Torah, an ancient text written over 3,300 years ago. No matter what religion you adhere to, whether you're an agnostic or a believer, we can all glean some truth from ancient Biblical stories that have been around since the year 1312 BCE. How did these heroic figures tackle the unknown? How did they forge ahead without anxiety or fear, so they could step into the next episode of life with unwavering faith? What methods did they use to become whole versus an empty vessel?

The very first man who discovered monotheism was Abraham. After Abraham made this discovery, Abraham was charged with a task. In the exact text it is written, "The Lord said to Abram, "Go forth from your native land and from your father's house to the land that I will show you." Why was Abraham asked to leave his comfort zone? In the following directive, God said to Abraham, if you leave, "I will make you a great nation. I will bless you, I will make your name great and you shall be a blessing."

God tasked Abraham to leave his comfort zone to discover his greatness. He was asked to leave everything he knew—his father, his birthplace, his home. Abraham forged into the unimagined.

For it is in the unimagined the imagination finally lives and breathes to tell its own story. It was only once Abraham made the decision to go into the wilderness without knowing what was next, that his life became blessed. We think of uncertainty as a cursed place because we're really good at telling ourselves stories. We imagine that there's danger lurking. But isn't it more dangerous to never take the leap to discover the unimaginable? Didn't I owe it to myself to take the leap of faith with courage versus with fragility? The pandemic had us making the biggest leaps of all socially, educationally, financially, religiously, and politically. It had us re-evaluating every sector of how we live life. And it forced us to re-evaluate our priorities in all these categories. Adjusting ourselves to this new normal made room for another normal. Maybe an even better, more present normal. Could I forge into that new normal that was presenting itself with grace?

When the pandemic came roaring through our cities, everything was disrupted. The way we interact, the way we pray, the way we shop, the way we vote—it was all crippled. Even our history—the formation of America, her values—was re-examined.

If we can suspend our negative Fox News/CNN thinking for a minute, we can clearly see that a reorganization in this world has begun. Like Abraham, we have been pushed into the wilderness. And the question we must ask ourselves is: Are we going to go? Or are we going to stay so frozen in our comfort zone—so scared to move, change, and adapt that we miss the opportunity to re-imagine our lives with a new fervor?

During the Persian Empire, around the fourth century BCE, a king by the name of Achashverosh (Ahasuerus) ruled the land. After he had his queen killed for not following orders, he took a Jewish woman by force to be his new queen. Queen Esther was told to keep her identity hidden, as the king was known to be threatened by the former Jewish monarch. At that time, the Jews who had ruled Jerusalem had been conquered by the Greeks and exiled. They found refuge in Persia, but King Achashverosh always felt their presence threatened his rule. Achashverosh believed the prophesied seventy years of the Jewish exile would end in the third year of his reign. When that time came and nothing happened, he was thrilled and believed the Jews would remain his subjects, without ever regaining power and independence. At the same time, Haman, the king's advisor, believed the only way to cement the king's rule was to annihilate the Jewish presence. He was threatened by the former superpower who had once ruled the Middle East. A plan had been set into motion by Haman, with the king's permission, to wage war against the Jewish community and wipe them out.

There are ancient texts that reference Mordechai being a Jewish diplomat in the King's court and head Wine Pourer (which was a highly esteemed position). He begged his cousin (some opinions say she was his wife), Queen Esther, to intervene and use her influence and charm to reverse the king's decree.

The problem was, Esther was scared to approach the king. She was the queen, but a queen who was taken hostage. She was little better than a slave. To top that, all the king's courtiers and the ladies of the court knew that if any person—man or woman—entered the king's inner court without being summoned, the law called for certain death. Esther entering the court of her own volition, without a formal invitation by the king, could have meant immediate execution—even though she was the queen.

If the king extended his gold scepter to the queen, she would live. If he withheld the scepter, she would die. Esther grappled with this difficult decision. In short, she explained to Mordechai that she had not been summoned by the king in the last thirty days. She begged Mordechai not to ask her to walk into uncertainty. *You're asking me to go on a suicide mission*, is basically what Esther feared.

Then Mordecai tells Esther, "Do not imagine that you, of all the Jews, will escape with your life by being in the king's palace. On the contrary, if you keep silent in this crisis, relief and deliverance will come to the Jews from another quarter, while you and your father's house will perish. And who knows—perhaps you have attained the royal position for just such a crisis."

Mordechai pointed out two things. He told Esther to recognize that either scenario had the potential for doom. She had already been kidnapped; she was already living an unpredictable fate. Eventually, the king would find out who Esther was, and she would still be a dead woman walking. He also pointed out that if she approached him, at least she'd be doing something, versus sitting like a victim, waiting for the end just doing nothing. Mordechai was encouraging Esther to take action and not become a victim. He was also pointing out the most important factor: We never know why we are sent into a situation. Or why we arrive in an ER on the busiest night of the year. We never know how we can be of service if we don't pay attention and ask ourselves, *what am I doing here and who needs my help?*

After weighing both options, Esther told Mordechai, "Go assemble all the Jews who live in Shushan." In other words, she said, this is not just about me. This is about the entire community coming together. She requested they fast on her behalf. And she ended her message to Mordechai by saying, "If I perish, I perish." She was willing to live with the outcome by leaning into the action. In that moment, Esther took back her freedom through her own resolve. She made her own decision to surrender to action versus action and through that act, she found her voice. A slave is a person who puts herself inside her own bondage by never desiring to wake up, who stays inside her own cocoon of shame, guilt, and sadness. Esther woke up that day and left the cocoon.

Esther decided to be bold in the midst of her uncertainty. She demanded a collective prayer session, where everyone was encouraged to take ownership of their decree. She asked that the larger community become her partner in stepping into a tenuous and uncertain situation.

That says so much about how to tackle uncertainty when there is a threat to a collective group. Esther leaned into her highest value, which was to create a united community to confront God through prayer and humility when there was so much at stake. I had to ask myself, "What am I doing to make myself vulnerable and allow others in to help me waver through?" In some ways I was afraid to say anything out loud, because to admit that your husband is dying would have made it all too real. It was easier to pretend things were 'fine' even though asking for collective prayer was my only chess move on the table. Lucky for me, I had some great role models for embracing vulnerability in the most vulnerable hour.

Years ago, I produced a short film for a series called "The Search," which was created by Filmmaker Marc Earlbaum, the founder of Nationlight Productions. The idea behind the series was to share how people found meaning. As the head of the West Coast production team, I was charged with asking celebrities, writers, radio hosts, philosophers, and thinkers the biggest human question out there: "What is the meaning of life?"

One night, there was a knock at my door. Our friend, Jeffrey, from our Synagogue, was standing outside. "I need to talk to you, Chava. Can I come in?" His shoulders were slouched, and his normally booming voice fell to a whisper.

Jeffrey proceeded to share that his baby daughter had just been diagnosed with a malignant tumor in her abdomen. The survival rate was extremely uncertain. Yet what Jeffrey said next changed the way I would come to think about this family forever.

"We are certain Zoe has cancer, but we are also certain that she will survive. *We got this.*"

Within weeks we had set up shifts for the family, making sure they had ongoing support. Jeffrey invited me to tell their story on camera, and his mantra continued to be "We got this," which became the title of the short film we made. Jeffrey and his wife, Ravit, leaned in to uncertainty with full positivity. Their entire approach to uncertainty was to beat it at its own game with certainty. That approach was risky. What if things didn't turn out the way they had hoped? How would they cope then? I questioned Jeffrey's approach. How many families had I known who had wished for positive outcomes but didn't get them?

Jeffrey's positive approach was contagious. But he also took the lead from Queen Esther, and called for community action to seal the deal. Believing the shift toward the miraculous can only happen through action, the night before Zoe's big surgery, the entire community gathered in collective prayer. People from several different counties made it their business, just as the Jews in Shushan two thousand years prior had made it theirs, to pray for the positive outcome that Jeffrey and Ravit were determined to find. The surgery was a success. Zoe is a healthy preteen now and is cancer free.

Jeffrey and Ravit did not just hold on to the positive outcome, they became a positive force that united communities around cancer awareness, helping others, praying for one another, and finding common ground. Do you know how many people I knew during that time who were wearing "I Got This" bracelets? Thousands. The wave of positivity that had been put in motion was addictive. I truly believe it became a pathway to end the Feldman's suffering around their child's illness. Their mighty approach allowed them to lean in to the discomfort with courage. They were not denying the pain or the anguish, they were just tackling it rather than cowering underneath it.

I am more than well aware that there are many stories that don't end with the outcome we wish for. I had time to pray earnestly for my own father's recovery. I prayed all the way to the hospital with my six siblings, my sister-in-law, and my husband. What I would have given to stop time.

We were not able to shift that story through prayer or manifest a positive outcome. Several minutes after walking into the ICU, my father took his last breath. We never saw it coming.

Yet, I am still encouraged to use my audacity to cling to hope, especially when hope is all we have. As Rabbi Jonathan Sacks wrote in his book *Morality*:

"Shame and necessity give rise to a culture of tragedy. Guilt, repentance and responsibility give rise to one of hope. ... There is no fate that is inevitable, no future predetermined, no outcome we cannot

avert. There is always a choice. There are tragic cultures and there are hope cultures, and, though some combine elements of both, the two are ultimately incompatible. In hope cultures we are agents. We choose. …The choice of freedom brings the defeat of victimhood and the redemptive birth of hope."

In Queen Esther's story, the outcome was no less miraculous. Upon her approach to the king's court, without an invitation, she won the King's heart and he did indeed extend the gold scepter, saving her and the Jewish people. What's beautiful about Queen Esther and about Jeffrey and Ravit Feldman is that they leaned in to valuing life. They were not married to the outcome; they were married to the action. The action of choosing to defeat victimhood through birthing hope.

At the time, I thought Jeffrey and Ravit's approach was too risky. But the truth is, not having that approach would have been riskier. They bet on using positivity to shift their story. No matter what their outcome, they had already won. Of course they wanted a great outcome. They were parents! But they were also determined to battle valiantly, no matter what the cost. They defeated their victimhood by choosing a hope mentality. Their attitude of positivity still continues to this day. Jeffrey even gave back by donating his own kidney to a child in need a few short years after their daughter's miraculous recovery.

When we're in this tidal wave of uncertainty, and we don't know what tomorrow brings, let's realize that we can be even more frightened and in more pain by doing nothing. The "what ifs" we make up can keep us stuck in a place of fear. Sometimes it does feel like there is nothing we can do to change what is frightening us. But I always think there's a little something we can all do; there are little tiny micro decisions that can make things better, so everything eventually becomes okay.

After my father died, I chose to make these little tiny micro decisions every single day. To me, the meaning of life is connecting with others, finding our light and our creative action, and keeping our will focused on our little tiny micro decisions. I had two choices, crawl into my bed and pretend the loss never happened, or write it all down and face my fears, regrets, my loss and devastation. That year I wrote a memoir that I believe got me through the worst time of my life. I wrote and recorded several songs. My creativity eventually led to the film project I got to work on with Jeffrey and Ravit. Two years later, standing in Jeffrey and Ravit's home I got to ask them, "What is the meaning of life?" I chose to keep on hoping. I chose to show up to life even when my outcome was not optimal. That choice saved my life.

The question we must ask ourselves when the uncertainty chokes us is, what small choice can I make today that will make tomorrow more positive, joyful, and connected to the people around me? The question I had to ask myself before falling asleep the night before my husband's procedure was, "Am I willing to invite others into this process and pray with us? Could I allow myself to step into the next minute with the audacity that Esther had, the imagination that Abraham acquired and the positive fierceness that Jeffrey and Ravit inhabited? These were lessons I was so blessed to have been given before this crisis roared through our lives. I believe the decision we made to walk through this with our community, smiling through the pain yet still acknowledging the fear was our saving grace.

After the Doctor announced Robbie's serious condition, did I have the audacity to say "We Got this," or not? Would I pay attention to the finer reasons why we ended up in this particular foreign hospital away from our home, in a foreign city with little resources? Would I have the gall to walk through each moment with a little more faith and a lot less victimhood? I had a choice to make in how I was going to move into the next moment and how we would tackle the biggest obstacle we faced as husband and wife yet. Essentially I had to decide if I wanted to lean into a tragic culture or a hopeful one. That decision would ultimately be the key to walking through the next disorienting door confidently versus powerlessly.

PART 2

HEALING RELATIONSHIPS DURING THE CRISIS

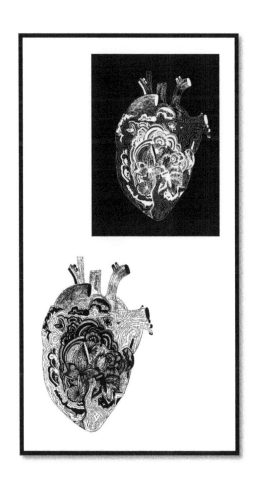

CHAPTER 5

BEING MARRIED
TO A RABBI

Throughout the years, many people have asked me, "What *IS* it like being married to a rabbi?" That answer has morphed many times for me over the years. As a rabbi's wife, people often refer to me as "rebbetzin," which is the feminine Yiddish adaptation of the word rabbi. I am also referred to as a "rabanit," which is the Hebraic version of the word rabbi. For a rabbi to be called a rabbi, one needs at least seven years of rabbinical study coupled with a very in-depth Talmud background. For a woman to be called rebbetzin, she basically just needs to say "I do" under a canopy to a rabbi.

I have never felt really comfortable being called rebbetzin; it always felt like a response to someone else's accomplishments versus a title given to me for my own personal achievement. I remember the first time someone used that term to refer to me. When my husband ran a day school, one of the dads called to let him know his child had "left his backpack in the rebbetzin's car." Neither of us could understand for the life of us why that was our problem, until it dawned on both of us that the rebbetzin the dad referred to was—me.

My relationship with this title has been an ever-evolving transition, as it was difficult for me to adopt a title without merit. My husband worked for over ten years to achieve the title of rabbi under a grueling regimen of Talmudic study. While I did spend years in Jewish study through high school, and another year after that in seminary, and though I have continued my studies throughout the years and have never stopped learning, I didn't feel entitled to its sister label just because I chose to marry well.

Being married to a rabbi is sort of like this. Imagine you're a patient getting prepped for surgery, but before the surgeon makes the first incision, the doctor's wife arrives saying, "Hi, here's a brisket, I will be present upon your return from surgery to listen to your deepest secrets and be of emotional service to you in every capacity. I might even point out to the doctor how he could perform your nephrectomy more optimally. (Even though I have never studied how to perform surgery specifically in depth, after being married to Dr. Stein this long I may have figured out some creative ways to remove your kidney just as efficiently.) By the way, are you single? Because I might know someone. Oh, and call me doctorette."

Yeah, it's kind of like that.

Watching *The Crown* became the touching point for me to finally accept the title of rebbetzin. Having that title is not just given by the mere fact that you married well. Rather, I see it as a privilege versus a right. Much like a queen or a first lady, being a rabbi's wife comes with an oath and a duty to be in a partnership, to be of service to others. If a queen protects the monarchy, and the first lady protects democracy, then I have finally come to understand that it is a rebbetzin who protects the Jewish faith. And not just for herself, but for her husband, her congregation, and especially for her children. For isn't living alongside faith at times comparable to forging into battle? There's a reason it's called practicing faith and not performing faith. A practice takes time, devotion, lots of pit stops, some falls, and regular questioning.

So what IS it like being married to a rabbi? To really answer that, I'll need to give you a deeper understanding of what drew me to marry one.

I can remember the very first date we had when I was nineteen years old and he was a twenty-three-year-old, bright-eyed rabbinical student.

It was July when our budding romance began. Robbie was the first boy I had ever dated. My mother told me he would be taking me to a hotel at 9 p.m., then she handed me a new blouse and said, "It's silk, not polyester. Wear it." *Good*, I thought, *at least the blouse won't feel cheap.*

A hotel at 9 p.m. might seem shady, but think of it like *Bridgerton* without the grand balls; when it came to Orthodox Jewish courtship, private-yet-public was how we rolled. We met at The Ritz Carlton in Laguna Hills after being set up by the matchmaker. The date took place in a remote hotel, which balanced private (because he was driving me an hour away, and the likelihood of running into anyone we knew was nil), and public, because we had strict instructions to stay in the lobby. As for the late hour? This student rabbi had not gotten permission from his head principal and was breaking out to pick me up. A rebel rabbi—I was already intrigued.

He pulled up in a black Lincoln Town Car. His friend, Nelson, owned a car rental company, so he was given a range of luxury vehicles from which to choose. Rebellious and innovative: check and check.

He showed up in a classic blue suit, which I would later learn was the only suit he owned, and got out of the car to open the door for me. Chivalry was not lost, at least with him. "Don't look now," he said, "but the matchmaker is standing behind those garbage cans making sure I pick you up in my black hat [customary Chassidic garb], which is exactly why I'm not wearing it tonight. The matchmaker asked to join us. I hope it's okay with you—I told him that wasn't happening."

The overprotective rabbi peering out from behind the garbage cans had been my second-grade teacher. My mother insisted we use him as the matchmaker even though I'd told my father I wanted to date Robbie six months prior. Mom didn't think it was appropriate to meet the yeshiva boy with the English name without an appropriate broker. "What kind of name is Robbie? It hardly sounds Jewish! Is his mother Jewish? We need to hire a rabbinic private eye," she ranted. (Little did I know, she actually had. Hence the rabbi peering out from the alley as I entered my first date.)

I got in the car with my homemade cinnamon buns and the excuse that the long drive might make us hungry. I brought baked goods like I was selling my homemaker skills in the most awkward interview. He often says that sealed the deal for him, and complains I haven't made them since. Cinnamon buns are the most difficult dessert to bake. I still wonder why I didn't bring easy rice krispy treats. (Note to self, tell my daughter not to make complex baked goods for a first date.)

The conversation was easy, like I had known him my whole life. We had many of the same acquaintances and experiences. He'd had more experiences, of course, because he was four years older. He stared at me with great concentration while I spoke. At one point he got out to help an old woman who fell crossing the street. The drive lasted two hours because we sat through most of the red lights for multiple cycles as he stared at me, listening intently, hanging onto every word I uttered. I thought it was charming and funny that I had captivated his attention enough to disrupt his driving.

At the hotel, ordering a stiff drink to calm my nerves was off limits given that I was only nineteen. We settled on ordering two Cokes, at $10 each. It was the most expensive soda he had ever purchased. I didn't finish my drink. The thought of telling him I had to pee completely disturbed me. He couldn't know just how human I was.

At the end of the night he turned to me and said, "Chava, you need to know something about me." At that point, the cynic in me was sure he was going to tell me about some hidden family mental illness. Instead, he said, "Chava, I am not possessed by the desire for wealth or acquiring money. I want to change the world through acts of service. I promise I will always take care of you, but I don't care to be rich in the conventional approach to living my best life. I care to be wealthy with deep, loving connections as we forge through our adventure together."

I came home that night to my mom, who had been waiting up with bated breath, full of questions. "Did you like him? Was there a connection? Do you want a second date?"

Worried I'd be poor and hungry if I married a man with such idealism, I shared with her what he'd said. She took a long pause and said, "Oh, what does he know. He's in rabbinical school. Once he marries you, he'll see how much you like to spend on shoes and he'll change his mind."

Five weeks later, I said yes. Twenty-eight years later, he is still rebellious and innovative and my best friend.

With better reflection, I have come to realize the term *rebbet-sin* does not actually mean I'm the person carrying the rabbi's sins. I have enough on my plate just carrying all of my own. No, the root word in rebbetzin comes from the word rabbi, which means to teach. We are charged to teach one another so that eventually we can share those teachings with others. This is scary. It means we have to live audaciously self aware. We have spent years mirroring one another's experiences, processing them alone, then processing together so we can eventually share our findings.. We are the true lab rats in existence. We have done this well and we have done this terribly. But we have fought through life practicing it just the same.

At the beginning of our marriage, my husband was not a rabbi in the conventional sense of the word. He did not have a congregation; he practiced his rabbinical service in the form of what he liked to call "street ministry." Meaning, he devoted his life to being of service to those around him versus having a formal congregation.

My husband has described his spiritual endeavor to lead as a journey similar to a scavenger hunt. He believes that since God places us in this world without clear direction (since none of us are born with a manual), we are left to discover our social responsibility assignments using the clues left by the patterns in our life. Both Robbie and I believe there are opportunities the Universe delivers to every one of us, yet it is our job to stay open and ready to decipher them. As my husband has put it, "Every opportunity starts with one word: Hello. If I don't say hello, then I can't possibly know why those people have been put in my universe. Some of the relationships I have been fortunate to have because of the 'Hello' have turned out to be deep, meaningful connections. Sometimes I can help that person, sometimes they can help me, sometimes we can help a third person." That statement pretty much sums up the answer of what it's like to be married to a rabbi. It's sort of like being married to the mayor of the town, where everybody knows your name and they're always glad you came.

CHAPTER 6

NURTURING RELATIONSHIPS

"Chava, we need to work on the way you communicate to Robbie. It is dripping with anger, like you want to hurt him."

"I do want to hurt him," I blurted out uncensored to my marriage therapist during our pandemic quarantine therapy. Before Robbie got sick, we had some things to work out. I don't know if I really wanted to hurt Robbie as much as I wanted him to feel my hurt, our hurt, his own hurt. I wanted him to feel something, anything that resembled the pain I was carrying around.

There was something looming over us as we approached empty nesting. For months I was trying to figure out how to re-engage in a marriage that felt like it had slipped into a coma. According to Robbie, everything was perfect. This was just a rough patch we would eventually get through. I felt like I was consistently shaking him to notice how broken we were (I was), only to be met with a resistance that was so exhausting. It became easier to live in his pretend world, even if it cost me my sanity. I really wanted us to face the music. But he didn't even notice the radio was blaring.

I tend to look at life like it's going to hell, whereas he loves to see that life has possibility. I should have known I married an optimist upon waking up on the first morning of our married bliss to find him whistling. At six a.m.—WHISTLING. I don't do whistling, and I don't do six a.m. Now imagine both of those coordinated efforts colliding simultaneously. And that's marriage in a nutshell. Learning to live with someone you love and need, and who loves and needs you, while simultaneously becoming the person who learns to love yourself, all while standing in the wreckage holding the hand of the person you love and love to hate all at once. It's a messy business, marriage, isn't it? For some it comes easy. I don't know those people, but I hear they might exist.

I came from a home where we yelled for attention. There were slammed and broken doors, tear-stained journals splayed across our beds. My dad would make us sit down during twelve-step meetings that ended in heart-to-heart battles with one of us eventually storming off. We entered that torture chamber regularly. Like champions in the arena, we battled valiantly. That was the practice. You could say anything you wanted. You could even storm out, but you had to show up.

On the opposite side of the spectrum, Robbie came from a family where big feelings were concealed. Those "I'm dying" talks, "Let's figure out how you feel about it," were not spoken about during the twelve years my father-in-law battled cancer. People said "I love you" with non-dramatic formality. Speaking from the heart was admired but also reserved. Robbie had become excellent at saying what he felt as long as he could censor himself. I did not even know the pathway to censorship. I had been trained amongst verbal Spartans, using words to cut my enemy down. While he had been trained amongst political adversaries who used silence and manipulation to puncture. We became excellent in battle with one another. We just needed to become better at loving one another. It was easier to ignore our hurts. We had experienced hurts before, like the pain of loss after our dads died. But the loss we were experiencing of empty nesting felt insurmountable. We love being parents. We love parenting together. What would we do once our kids left home? Man, this was scarier than the thought of either of us dying.

It became easier and easier to use our hurting as an excuse to turn away from one another than as our catalyst of turning toward one another. We became mirrors of our hurts instead of the place we went for refuge.

Then the pandemic hit. It hit us after a series of losses, years of financial devastation, my parents' divorce, burying our fathers, helping to raise four of my siblings alongside our own three children, marrying off several of my siblings, sending two of our three kids off to college, and all that comes with empty nesting that a twenty-five-plus-year marriage weathers. In the early part of our marriage I almost died a couple of times, had a cancer scare, a pregnancy that nearly cost me my life, eleven years of dealing with secondary infertility, then being told there was no hope for a fourth child. Robbie was never really sick a day in our marriage except the post-op infection he got after a hernia surgery that went a bit awry but was eventually resolved. Notice how small I make his complicated surgery sound and how massive I can make my own sound. He can sit in pain and never complain. I need the entire world to know my body is broken so they believe I might not make it and then I can invite everyone to my "*This could have been my funeral*" party, with the theme *"Now tell me again how much and why you all love me."*

For the most part, aside from constant migraines and definitely slowing down, Robbie was in pretty good shape. Sure, those seven-mile walks he started during lockdown began to wane, but I just figured he needed that vacation we so desperately put on our summer calendar. I knew that what we had faced as a married couple was not new. Plenty of couples have dealt with crisis and challenge. Like many couples, we did crisis quietly in our own battlefield on an epic scale and we made it look easy. It was hard AF. There was nothing simple about what we had endured. But we were the lucky ones, because we stayed together. Neither one of us abandoned the ship(wreck). Neither one of us died in the shipwreck either. We were both still in love. We both adored each other. He was my best friend and I was his. Up until our Las Vegas vacation, no one was dying. We were just dying inside. We became excellent maskers. It was the raft we held on to, which sank the very day we arrived on our much-needed vacation. Have I mentioned HOW MUCH I (*okay we*) NEEDED THAT VACATION? There was dis-ease and then finally disease. It felt like finding yourself suddenly on a haunted pirate ship, and just when you adjust your mind to that crazy, you realize you're about to sail into a volcano without pants on or a parasol to protect you from the falling ashes.

Apathy is the unwillingness to even acknowledge pain and difficulty. I have never wanted to live in apathy. I want to be awake and to notice the things that hurt. The way to cure disease is to first notice the symptom, then diagnose the problem, and then finally to heal the ailment. In our case, my response to our ongoing dis-ease was to react. Robbie's response was to retreat. But we were both actively responding with symptoms. However, when Robbie became septic and was then diagnosed with a broken heart, in some ways that was our gift. The gift we needed to move past the symptom into the diagnostics where we would finally arrive at the place of healing. Little did I realize the healing was beginning way before he got sick. It began in March 2020, when a pandemic loomed and a congregation needed our direction and our guidance on how to couple and partner better just as distractions fell to the wayside.

So no, I didn't really want to hurt Robbie, I just wanted to stop the hurting. Hurting him never made me feel less hurt. But I didn't have any tools in my toolbox, and so the tune up began.

The night before Robbie's heart procedure, my husband wrote goodbye letters to me and our children.

"There is no me without you. I love you so much. I pray God makes it all go well tomorrow. But if He has other plans, just know that because of you, life has already far exceeded my greatest expectations. If I could do it all again with the foreknowledge of all to come, I would do it all again with you. I would just do it even better."

The following day, I kissed my husband goodbye as they wheeled him into the operating room. I entered the meditation room to pray. I needed to be okay with any outcome. I needed to know I could hear the calling to the other side should my husband land there. I needed to be certain my relationship with him was beyond time, place, and the corporeal world.

"Dad," I prayed, "Give me a little sign from above that you have my back. That we're not alone on the pirate ship."

I needed to know that if Robbie lived or died, we would still remain connected. I would still be okay. As I waited for Robbie in his hospital room to come back to me, Nicole, a student nurse who had never been to our hospital, was put on our rotation and asked if I needed anything.

"Nicole, thank you for being here. Where are you from?" I asked.

"I'm from Sacramento," she replied.

As soon as Nicole said she was from Sacramento, I got that tingle. A knowing crept inside my body and shuddered into intuitive electric shocks which announced that sign from above had finally arrived.

"You mean you're from Chico," I stated very matter-of-factly back.

"Chico is nearly three hours north of Sacramento. How did *you* know that I was from that exact town?" she asked.

I knew Nicole was from Chico because that was the city where my late father had been hired to be the head gastroenterologist eighteen months before he died. It was also where he took his last breath, and where my older brother was born. Chico is significant to our family story. It is a small town. Knowing my dad sent a nurse from that city made me realize he was absolutely watching over us.

Robbie made it out of the procedure with confirmed endocarditis, a heart infection coupled with another life-threatening heart issue. A mitral valve regurgitation, flailed leaflet, torn chordae, and what appeared to be ninety percent arterial blockage, which meant that his heart was not beating, it was hissing. Two weeks later, our cardiologist eventually discharged us saying, "We're sending you home in a pique line to your heart with ongoing IV antibiotics for the next six weeks. You have five hours to get back to Los Angeles before your next dose. Missing it could be fatal. Your heart is only working at twenty percent capacity. Just don't die."

It would take four hours to drive back to Los Angeles on a good day. Back at the hotel, a friend sensed my nervous energy and booked me a massage to prep for the white-knuckle drive home. After the treatment, Kevin, the therapist said in his calming voice, "On July twenty third, two thousand and one, I was in a massive car accident off Cherry and Lakewood Street in Long Beach, California. I almost died, but I survived, and now that you are fully relaxed, I'm sure you'll be okay too."

My father died on July twenty third, and he practiced medicine in a hospital for thirty years off that exact intersection in Long Beach where Kevin almost died, but didn't. Another sign that dad was watching. Another sign he had our backs.

Nicole's family owned a nut farm in Chico. The farm's motto? 'We're all nuts.' Well, the situation sure felt nuts. But my reaction to handling this crisis knowing that I would be okay despite any outcome was not nuts.

So how do you say EGBOK when you've wandered into the bottomless pit? The key to the EGBOK attitude implies things aren't okay right now. Saying *everything's going to be okay* gives you permission to call the present moment horrible.

My dad, Dr. Mike, who was a gastroenterologist, used to say, "Treat the patient, not the disease." In this case, I had to learn how to treat this intolerable moment with gentleness, and treat the future with hope.

Whenever I'd hear about one of my father's patients being terminal I'd ask, "How much longer does he/she have?" And every time my father's response would be the same, "Only God knows."

"Yes, but how much time?" I'd probe. I knew other doctors would give their patients the amount of time they had left—a week, three months, two years...yet my father always refused. He never indulged in such cruelty. In his mind, time was a daily practice to be handled with gentleness and not to be thrown around like a race for the finish line.

We often think of hope as this withering flower to be preserved behind glass. A cloud we cannot grasp, which is anemically delicate. Hope is made by clawing through blood and mud, sweat and tears, after forging through thorns—on a good day. Hope is forged through grit and steel. "Everything is going to be okay," was my father's way of not avoiding the inevitable. It was welcoming the possibility that every second we are breathing was an invitation to engage. So no, he would never give a patient a timetable to their life just to ruin their last precious moments.

To honor the truth of the experience is the most important factor in making it up the next difficult ramp. Acknowledging the truth of the current moment is what gives you the audacity to accept the next one with hope. How we shape this present moment is how we shape our guided future. It is "*going*" to be okay…meaning, while you are in the heavy, you can still muster up the courage to bet on your resilience. You don't have to sit at that blackjack table of distraction called fear. *It is going to be okay* is betting on yourself. It is betting on your ability to stand in the storm without it decimating your soul. *It is going to be okay* is the pathway toward finding your true inner voice, not listening to the whispers saying you can't withstand the crisis. It is giving yourself the opportunity to not bet on outcome as the key to your survival, but to bet on your ability to withstand any outcome, optimal or not, with fortitude, boldness, and daring nerve.

For me, the key to our healing as husband and wife and to Robbie healing from his life-threatening illness was to stay in the moment. To honor our ability to move through this difficult challenge. To notice we have done hard stuff together before, and we will do the hard stuff together again. I still needed better tools. It is a good thing I had a few in my toolbox, which is exactly what I got after conducting the many interviews on the Nurture Series podcast, or I would had never learned to love my life 90 seconds at a time, as author Joan Rosenberg taught me in her book, *90 Seconds To A Life You Love* amongst other wonderful authors and coaches I was fortunate enough to interview. But to understand how this podcast came into being, we must begin with a Costco fiasco.

CHAPTER 7

HEALING OUR RESILIENT SELVES

As the Pandemic began, my husband and I both realized that with services canceled, we needed to pivot the way we serve. We lead a young professional congregation, mostly between the ages of twenty and forty. Our congregants are either single, dating, engaged, or newlyweds. Three weeks after lockdown, the calls began pouring in. There were folks announcing quick engagements and even quickie weddings. One call was from a newly engaged couple who'd had plans to wed in six months, but who ultimately decided, after living apart during a quarantine with an unforeseeable future, to get married the following day. My husband was wary their decision was too hasty and not well thought out. And then I reminded him how he asked me to marry him, on the eve of the holiest fast of the year, the holiday of Yom Kippur, merely five weeks and eleven dates after our first meeting.

"Love is love," I said. I found the gesture of this young couple marrying within forty-eight hours—on their parent's driveway with a Zoom set up for all their guests—romantic, and a perfect expression of how to live life: like every second counts.

But then came the other calls. The barrage of young couples who had been struggling to get along, who were considering divorce. They had begun questioning their early decisions to forge through life as a couple after finding themselves in quarantine, forced to look at their broken relationships without the host of distractions that pre-pandemic life provided. There were also the happy couples overwhelmed by daily life as they now found themselves caring for their small children 24/7, without outside help or school to break up the day, which now caused their happy marriages to enter a state of uncertainty. That brought on a host of communication issues, intimacy disruptions, and other relationship challenges. There were fathers and mothers balancing work and home life in small apartments. There were couples who had relied on their social lives and were now forced to spend their waking hours alone without any other people to distract them or enrich their lives. The number of phone calls from those struggling couples was staggering.

They were looking at us for answers. And the work we needed to do on ourselves became evident during a Costco run.

At the height of the lockdown, Robbie suggested we run to Costco to make sure we had enough provisions. The shelves were emptying, toilet paper was dwindling, and the supply chain appeared shaky. Uncertainty ran high, and with it came a growing tension that was seeping into our interactions. We were several weeks into lockdown, when I recall feeling extremely stuck in the house. This made me grouchy. Little did I know I was also slowly slipping into menopause. I'm sure that cute hormone crusade didn't help my "lovely" mood, which my dear husband was about to experience in the wine aisle.

I had agreed to go along on the Costco outing but hadn't expressed my real need to Robbie: I needed to be outdoors. I felt locked inside and I wanted the beach—an expanse, an experience to clear my mind and get more centered. I figured I would share that goal with Robbie eventually, but by the time we hit the Vodka and Merlot display, I was struggling. That was my first mistake. I failed to tell Robbie what I needed with kind-hearted directness before joining the Costco field trip. And then it happened: we got to the lox section and Robbie got that I-love-Costco-with-all-my-heart-this-is-the-best-store-in-the-world-let's-spend-all-day-here kind of look. But again, instead of using my voice to express my real need—outside, expanse—I didn't take into account how thrilled he was to be in Costco and said, "Babe, let's just get in and get out. Let's not make this an all-day event." Robbie was deeply disappointed. One does not just *"get in and get out"* of Costco. One lingers. One dreams. Dare I say, one hunts like Indiana Jones on a mission to find the best markdown. Have I mentioned how much he loves Costco? At this point, the altercation was set like a countdown to a rocket launch. You know how you say one thing when you mean something else, which leads to your partner responding in ways you only hear as rude, which in the bubble above your head comes out as the-ten-things-about-you-that-suck? So hypothetically that may have led to the wife (aka me) storming out of Costco like a storm trooper raiding the Millennium Falcon. (I've chosen to use dated 1980s references in case you didn't catch that I was raised in the Madonna era.) Later, he admitted his response to my "Let's get in and get out" comment was not something he was proud of either. You can picture the epic battle that ensued.

The Nurture Series was born out of a necessity to become better teachers and spouses. My husband and I had created a host of Zoom classes on Biblical topics and other Jewish themes, but the one class everyone needed, the one class we needed the most was how to couple during a crisis.

Originally, *The Nurture Series* was envisioned as a three-part live series where dinner was delivered to our congregational couples (and in some cases a bottle of wine), at 8 p.m., after the children had gone to sleep. During dinner, the couples were invited to attend a Zoom interview which I conducted. It was important to me that these interviews included therapists, communication coaching experts, and clinicians who could give all of us sustainable tools to create lasting and loving relationships. The program became so successful that I decided to continue the series, interviewing experts on how to nurture ourselves within all areas and aspects of our lives. Those interviews can be found in the ongoing podcast *The Nurture Series*, which is available on iTunes and Spotify.

There were a couple of questions I kept asking myself. How do we have more effective partnerships during uncertain times? And how can we nurture our relationships in really healthy ways especially during a crisis and in the aftermath of one? When the pandemic first hit, many relationships entered an "intimacy lockdown." For many, intimacy was what we needed, but not what we were able to achieve. Robbie and I found ourselves struggling to maintain a connection among the constant barrage of fear and uncertainty. Now throw in a pandemic, a pending empty nest—and menopause—into the mix, and you got yourself a whole world of crazy. Fear is one of those divine emotions that, if we are not willing to tame into submission, can rule our lives and our relationships. It can cause reactions that disrupt our sense of peace and our deep connections.

In my first interview on *The Nurture Series*, clinical therapist Dr. Joan Rosenberg reiterated that the key to finding and maintaining a loving relationship is supporting each other's sense of safety. "Safety is the key to finding love," she said. Running out of Costco and abandoning the man I love during the experience he adores most had not exactly provided safety. Communicating with my cutting resentments did not provide a place of safety. It was up to me to heal my own hurts just as it was up to Robbie to heal his. Coming together meant helping one another through the pain and then using love as our battle cry versus our grievances. I had bad habits and I knew they needed to be amended. Healing for me was going to mean getting to the source of my pain.

Dr. Joan Rosenberg is a cutting-edge psychologist, consultant, and master clinician. She's also a best-selling author, and acclaimed speaker and trainer. She's a two-time TEDx speaker and a member of the Association of Transformational Leaders. She's been recognized for her thought leadership and influence in personal development. She mainly talks about how to achieve emotional, conversational, and relationship mastery, and how to integrate neuroscience and psychotherapy, even suicide prevention. Joan is a professor of graduate Psychology at Pepperdine University in Los Angeles and her latest book, *90 Seconds to a Life You Love: How to Master Your Difficult Feelings to Cultivate Lasting Confidence, Resilience, and Authenticity*, was released in February 2019. It has become my family's bible! No joke. She is an Air Force veteran, and her calm, level-headed approach to deciphering the trials of relationships has become a beacon of light for many struggling couples.

So, what is the hidden question that partners should really be asking each other? Joan's answer astonished me, and yet it was so simple. "The deepest question that partners should be asking of one another, whether they verbalize it or not, is, 'Will you be there for me?'"

The most important thing we can achieve in a relationship for the other person is to help them feel safe. If either of us were defensive or critical, then the other would experience that response as a lack of safety—which meant that had to change within both of our communication styles. I could not roll my eyes, I couldn't be hostile, I could not stonewall, "Because every one of those things would be experienced as a lack of safety," Joan said.

In *The Seven Principles for Making Marriage Work*, relationship expert Dr. John Gottman talks about the Four Horsemen, indicators of the end of a relationship. The Four Horsemen are criticism, contempt, defensiveness, and stonewalling.

Criticism is criticizing, denouncing, or condemning your partner. Contempt is hostility and disgust demonstrated as eye rolling or other aggression. Defensiveness is not really hearing the other person's complaint before setting up your own line of defense. And then stonewalling is completely withdrawing, detaching, and even using silence as a weapon. John uses the New Testament harbingers of the end of times to name these communication styles because, according to his research, they can predict the end of a relationship. How do we avoid the apocalypse?

The Costco meltdown was our tipping point. My reactions had become increasingly apocalyptic and super jumpy. The pandemic had started this avalanche of anxiety in so many of us, causing us to resort to the Four Horsemen. One wife shared with me that, "In order for me to get some distance from my husband, I have stopped letting him touch me by pretending to be asleep when he comes to bed." (Stonewalling.) There was a husband who admitted, "When I told my wife I needed more alone time with her, she reacted with a rant and instead of hearing my need, which would benefit both of us. She defended her actions rather than taking responsibility for ignoring our relationship." (Defensiveness.) Yet another couple called to let me know they didn't think they were ever really in love, which meant every interaction they participated in, he rolled his eyes, and she finished his sentences, and refused to let him speak his mind. (Contempt.)

There had to be healthy ways to connect that would help us lean into our relationships instead of damaging them. Dr. Joan Rosenberg helped us decipher our difficult emotions so that the Four Horsemen would not even have room to show up.

In the course of our conversation, she explained how uncertainty and terror leads to grief. As the world struggled with so much ongoing uncertainty it felt like "This was grief on top of grief," she said. We grieved what we lost, what we didn't know we would ever get back, and what we could not understand simultaneously. Those layers of grief had to be felt and acknowledged. Gone unchecked, they could also become our excuse for dissolving loving relationships. (I want to make clear that I'm not talking about unhealthy, toxic relationships. For some couples, divorce will be the answer. Not everyone is meant to be together, and I want to acknowledge that if you have discovered that in your relationship, these skills will still be just as important in uncoupling as they are for coupling.)

Joan shared a strong message for how to effectively communicate with our partners, create safety, and nurture trust through kind and well-intentioned communication. That message is exactly what we all needed in order to avoid the apocalypse. What are the guidelines for promoting this good connection in healthy relationships? "At no time is someone's integrity diminished. No mean words, no escalation, and there's no threat to the physical, mental, or emotional integrity of the other person...."

She went on to explain that "If there's a tone or there's an attitude, it doesn't warrant itself for connection. And that is when the breakdown begins." But how do we repair that connection if, say, you are at Costco and you lose it? I'm glad you asked, because there is a great answer.

Joan explained that often when we are having a breakdown in our relationship, it's not usually about the actual argument that is happening. It's usually about something else entirely. The key is to not be afraid and to "know what we know," as she so eloquently put it. "Most of us are afraid to know what we know." We are scared to see ourselves and so we put up those walls thinking no one will notice our fear or our frustrations. When really everyone notices the madness, especially our partners.

Robbie and I had clearly been afraid to know what we needed to know. We needed a relationship makeover and we couldn't be afraid to realize how damaging our four horsemen had become as they quietly rode in to dwell with us.

Arguments are usually about other things that couples are expressing in the relationship through body language, like rolling eyes or slamming doors—or, in my case, walking out on my partner during a much-needed field trip during lockdown. So whatever we were arguing about, the argument is usually deeper. Running underneath the conversation is resentment or frustration from other previous things. In my case, I was resenting the lockdown, exhausted by cooking and cleaning nonstop, stressed about reinventing my business, dealing with the fear of getting sick and the financial losses we were weathering, realizing my kids were about to leave home for good, which meant I needed to reinvent my sense of purpose, having unresolved grief I was excellent at ignoring.... It was all of it. But instead of sharing that, I kept responding with knee-jerk reactions. I lost my ability to be soft. I was ignoring some big feelings and some big emotions around my kids leaving, unresolved old grief, and frustrations in being able to access my personal sense of self.

Robbie and I have one rule which I truly believe has kept our relationship intact even when things felt unstable, and that is: there is never shame in a do-over. As much as I have been ready for a throw down, I am lucky to be with a partner who is always open for a do-over. And that has been our saving grace. So, how do we reset when in a relationship apocalypse?

Joan believes that with enough practice we can reset our reset. Meaning, we can train ourselves to never get to a place of escalation by regulating our bodies and being intentional with our authentic truth. The hint to discovering this truth lies in regulating our eight core uncomfortable feelings, which Joan believes we all inhabit. Resilience is the ability to allow these feelings to bleed into our consciousness and then tackle them with self-love and acceptance. Notice I didn't call these eight feelings good or bad. Because as Joan sees it, "The unpleasant feelings actually exist for our protection. They are neither good nor bad, they are merely uncomfortable." And how we stick in the discomfort is where we meet our resilience.

According to Joan, most of our argument breakdowns happen when we are fighting to avoid discomfort. "Mastering these eight difficult feelings is the foundational element toward building confidence and resilience, and actually living much more authentically. If you're living with more authenticity, then your relationships are going to skyrocket in terms of quality, or at least they have the potential to do that," shared Joan. **These eight uncomfortable feelings are: sadness, shame, helplessness, anger, vulnerability, embarrassment, disappointment, and frustration.**

Joan was careful to explain that these eight did not include resentment, guilt, anxiety, or even fear. Because according to Joan "these eight (feelings) are the most common everyday, spontaneous reactions to things not turning out the way we either perceive we need, or the way we want them to be."

When I left Costco in a ball of anger, I was mostly upset that I did not use my voice to let my partner know that I was overwhelmed by my lockdown feelings and by the growing wedge we managed to shove between ourselves. I was frustrated and scared about reinventing myself once our youngest son left for college. I was uncertain about our future. The pandemic was the last straw that pushed my anxiety into overdrive and made our future that much more uncertain. I felt frustrated and disappointed, but instead of sharing those feelings, I was afraid to know what I knew in that moment. I reacted by running away from how I felt. I was trying to avoid the unpleasant feelings. Had I been more attuned to myself, I could have expressed my disappointment and frustration to my partner with loving and well-intentioned dialogue. The key to tuning into those feelings is breath work. Taking a deep breath and just being aware of what those feelings are is the start to learning how to self-regulate. And once we master self-regulation, we can express what is actually going on in a well-intentioned, kind manner. Knowing this is a work in progress allows us to remain patient with ourselves even when we don't get it right.

I was curious if Joan felt there was a difference between the way those who lean into their masculine energy deal with their uncomfortable feelings versus those beings who are more grounded in their feminine energy. In general, Joan thought that people who lead with male energy have the tendency to hear feedback from those partners who operate from their female energy as criticism. She said that oftentimes, that can get translated into "I've done bad." And then "I've done bad" becomes "I feel bad," and "I feel bad" becomes "I am bad." Joan felt it was this tendency which caused male energetic beings to withdraw.

She suggested that female energetic beings can't really fix how male energetic beings receive the information, but they can become more mindful of their approach by avoiding the Four Horsemen. It's all about being mindful of technique. "Tone," she said, "…is everything. Part of what men have to do as listeners, if they want to change up this dynamic, when your partner is providing feedback, it's intended as information. It is not intended as a statement about you. You have to depersonalize the feedback. Say to yourself, 'I need to just hear it for the information.' Assume that she is saying it to you for your best interest, because she loves you, not because she wants to hurt you. Otherwise it gets mangled."

It's similar to the game telephone, where one person whispered one thing to another, and the whisper traveled around the group until the last person received a mangled message. For example, a wife could be saying one thing to her spouse, but the spouse might hear something else. To him, there is a different context and different subtext. He hasn't heard what his wife said, because there are all these other ideas and assumptions layered into it for him. That can start to make the tennis match of conversation feel difficult. Masculine energetic beings are sensitive to tone. It's best to avoid phrases like "You need to…" or "You have to…." They can be replaced with phrases like "I would love it if…" or "Would you please…?" Joan is a big believer that masculine energetic beings prefer directness. While in general, female energetic beings according to Joan, "…Have the tendency (generally, in my experience), to ask a question when they have a statement to make. And the guy's trying to figure out the answer, but gets the answer wrong. And now you're angry at him because the answer was incorrect."

Female energetic beings tend to jump through hoops trying to figure out different ways to tell our partners something. According to Joan, it really doesn't have to be that complicated. We could just say, "Hey, baby, I need some beach time to help ease my anxiety. I know you love it here, I'm so happy we came here together, but let's also catch some waves after we finish here." So why do we pull back from speaking our truth? It's the creative way we have concocted to dodge our emotional discomfort—or the emotional discomfort of our partners. The last thing I wanted to know was that I was a ball of anxiety. The last thing I wanted to feel was the discomfort of that knowing—or to feel his discomfort. Had I allowed myself to tune into what we were both feeling, how much better would that Sunday have gone? "We're more authentic when we allow ourselves to experience the whole range of our feelings. Speaking with comfort and ease with your partner has to do with your willingness to lean into experiencing those feelings. We tend to come to know what we're feeling emotionally through bodily sensation," reiterated Joan.

If we are not in tune with our bodies, or we have learned to detach from our core sensations, we may not even pick up on some of these bodily cues. We might not even know what emotion we are feeling. A big part of being a successful partner is being in touch with your own body, and really feeling what's going on inside.

For example, when I feel a sense of overwhelm, if any of those unpleasant feelings start to happen, it's right in my chest. I can feel my heart pounding, my face gets hot, and I start to feel like I can't breathe…a little panic might set in. I will do anything to avoid that feeling. And when I avoid it, the authentic self I know my partner enjoys connecting to leaves, and the she-devil replaces her. But when I breathe through the discomfort and I allow it to be there in all its glory, that's when my resilience kicks in. Then I can tap into truth and say what is on my mind with more ease and with a kind, loving approach. I don't have to rely on my formative training and respond like a Spartan EVERY time I feel overwhelmed. That's the 90-second reset that Joan's book is named for. The 90-second reset, or as she also calls it, "The Rosenberg Reset," is based on the concept that these emotions are short-lived. An emotion can only last in the body for 90 seconds. If we can weather the storm of how our body responds to sadness, shame, helplessness, anger, vulnerability, embarrassment, disappointment, and frustration, then we can really get through anything.

Being authentic means we can screw up without beating ourselves up over it. We have to come to terms with the fact that punishing ourselves for not getting it right the first time is just as harmful as getting it wrong.

Living with shame about making my Costco day a fiasco was not a healthy option. But neither was failing to own my part in it by ignoring that uncomfortable feeling. By failing to acknowledge my discomfort needed tending to, I was self-sabotaging. So try the 90-second reset. Get in tune with your uncomfortable feelings, and then let your partner know what you have discovered. What is your body really telling you? That is truly the best way to carve out authentic and healthy loving connections.

CHAPTER 8

NURTURING EFFECTIVE COMMUNICATION

Once we know what we are feeling, the next part is to actually communicate that feeling. That is not easy for many people. We are living in the age of texting, where communication has dwindled down to shorthand. Rarely do we take the time to communicate deeply and effectively with our partners. Communication does not just happen with our words. According to Jeff Thompson, Ph.D., in *Psychology Today*, "The belief is that 55% of communication is body language, 38% is the tone of voice, and 7% is the actual words spoken." That means that if we are relying solely on our words to get a point across, our communication is suffering immensely.

If the lockdown provided anything, it was time. Lots and lots of time to practice the art form of communication. It is ironic that we are social creatures who have lost the art of communicating effectively. Speaking to Dr. Joan Rosenberg on effectively communicating with our partners while creating safety and deeper connections had me wanting to interview a communication coach who knew how to put these ideals into practice. I interviewed Lauren Weinstein.

Lauren was really generous in demonstrating how she solves conflict. She got super vulnerable and shared with me areas she struggled in, and how she solved those struggles using positive communication.

Lauren Weinstein is a communications coach and consultant who helps her clients develop stronger relationships and more powerful communication skills. For five years, Lauren taught one of the most popular communication classes at the Stanford Graduate School of Business on the essentials of strategic communication. She has a very popular TED Talk, which I highly recommend, which is now approaching two and a half million views. Her articles on communication and relationships have been published in *Harvard Business Review* and the *HuffPost*. Lauren received her BA in psychology from Stanford University. She studied coaching and leadership development at the Coaches Training Institute.

A few years back, I was in a theater group. One of the improv games was called "Yes, *and*...." The idea behind the game is that one person builds a story and the second person continues building that experience by responding with "Yes, *and*...." Both parties are contributing with the intention that they are both on the same side. According to Lauren, the key to a successful relationship lies in creating a "Yes, *and…*" approach.

But what if you see something in your partner that warrants an improvement? Is there an effective way to critique our partners? What should the dialogue look like when we do have criticism to share? Lauren explained that language absolutely matters. "Rather than saying 'Oh, you need to fix this.' The words can be, 'I think it would really serve you…' or 'I think our relationship would be stronger if….'" For example, Lauren shared, "When I'm coaching someone for a public speaking gig, I might need to critique their approach. I might notice they need to be more animated to get their point across. So I would lead with saying, 'If you had more expansive gestures, or used your voice this way or that way, or told your story with more cadence, then you'd become more powerful.'"

Even just framing how we tell someone to see their power is more effective in sharing critique. And in an interpersonal relationship, starting with the purpose and clear intention of creating connection always softens the blow when a critique is in order.

It's not just about the language we use—it's also about the timing. Going back to my Costco fiasco, had I couched the invitation Robbie gave me before we left the house with my expectation for needing beach time, I could have completely avoided the lox aisle apocalypse. It's not like I wouldn't have been effective at sharing my need for beach time to Robbie while we were in the car on the way to Costco, or even upon arrival at the store; after all, I am married to a pretty reasonable person. But to take timing into account when he was under the same stress I was holding, and knowing that a Costco run was his way of letting out steam, all needed to be part of the equation in my communication process. Preparing him for a game change ahead of time would have been a much more effective way to communicate my needs while serving our connection with more compassion. It would have allowed him to manage his expectations and he might have been more willing to concede to my request.

I wanted Lauren to share an example of a conflict she might have had which she was able to trail blaze through using her communication methods. Lauren shared the following story.

"At work, I can really take charge, and I'm a coach and a leader. But interpersonally, I had a Jewish mother who was very opinionated and overbearing. While I love my mom—she's an amazing person— oftentimes, she would enforce her will, which had me going in the other direction. Because of that trigger, I always want to check in versus thrusting my own will onto my partner."

Lauren shared a particular conversation she had with one of her past boyfriends. Although they did not have any set plans, he had invited her to a certain event but the plans were not set in stone. She had waited and waited for him. In her last conversation with him, she had believed he would let her know if the plans were set in motion or not. But then she did not hear back from him and she wound up waiting around without any idea of what the plan was. He went to the event without her. She was extremely upset and realized she needed to use her voice to handle the misunderstanding.

As Lauren shared, "In my early days, I might have responded with stonewalling. Because that pattern started from my youth. My own nuclear family tended to be so intense, I went the other way, which meant I would withdraw and not communicate what I needed or felt. We all have needs, and if those needs are not met, we get triggered. We might feel upset, frustrated, tense, anxious. There's often a trigger, right? Somebody doesn't call you back, or somebody doesn't clean up their clothes, and it's at that moment we have to redesign the way our reaction might reflect the need we want—which is actually to be connected, to feel connection. Going back to my disappointment in my then-boyfriend for not calling me, it never led to a fight, because the way I said things didn't cause a fight-or-flight defensive reaction from him, because there was no attack. And while my normal reaction might have been to stonewall, instead I called him right away and I said "Hey, so when you didn't call me, I didn't feel great, I would have liked for the loop to have been closed on that conversation if you were going out, or if we were spending time together."

As a result of how Lauren used her voice in that scenario, she and her partner were both able to mend that particular miscommunication by being present and staying open, and they both came from a place of *"Yes, and…."* <u>*Yes*</u> *I want to hear what's wrong, <u>and</u> I'd love to repair it together.*

Now what happens if one of the Four Horsemen rears its head? What does that communication look like in comparison to a "Yes, and…" dynamic? Lauren gave a really great example around how two people might speak to one another using two of the Four Horsemen: Defensiveness and Stonewalling.

"This is a real conversation between my mother and grandfather that demonstrates how conversations actually took place in my family unit. These conversations lead to defensiveness, which is how I learned how to stonewall.

Mom: 'Dad, what's wrong with you?'

Grandpa: 'You never called me!'

Mom: 'I don't call you because whenever I do call you, you yell and criticize me.'

Grandpa: 'Well, I don't want to have this conversation with you. Because whenever I do, you are irrational, and I wouldn't yell and criticize you if you did things right.'

"Notice they both got very defensive in that exchange. Rather than get defensive, it would have been more helpful to take responsibility. If you deal with needs and feelings, you actually take ownership and responsibility and you share what's going on for you. So instead, the conversation could have looked like this:

"Mom: 'Dad what's wrong?'

"Grandpa: 'Why didn't you call?'

"Mom: 'I'm sorry I didn't call before. I feel sad because last time we spoke I felt criticized.'

"Grandpa: 'I'm sorry I criticized you. I feel sad and lonely. I really want to connect and feel included in your life.'

"Notice, that exchange would have created a less defensive reaction."

We all have different needs as partners. Many times we forget that fulfilling those needs can't be accomplished for one another if we don't even know what they are. Lauren shared that the best way to really understand how to support each other is by getting in tune with our love languages.

I remember reading the book *The Five Love Languages* by Gary Chapman many years ago. In the book, Gary explains the five love languages that human beings use to show our love and appreciation for one another. They are: 1. Words of affirmation (for example, telling your partner "I love you, I value you"). 2. Acts of service (for example: cooking, cleaning, bringing your partner coffee every morning). 3. Giving gifts. 4. Quality time. 5. Physical touch. You can take the quiz on Gary Chapman's website to find out what your love language is. It's a fun way to connect with your partner and start the discussion.

If you know what your partner's love language is, why is it sometimes so difficult to give or receive that language? The challenge lies in our comfort around being vulnerable. Not only with our partners, but even with ourselves. To be vulnerable, social scientist Brené Brown writes, "is at the core, the center for meaningful human experiences." She also writes that "Vulnerability is not about winning, and it's not about losing. It's about having the courage to show up and be seen."

Lauren shared that the best way to overcome vulnerability is to "Just ask for it, directly." Not as a demand, but as a means to promote loving connection.

Joan had shared in her interview with me that using humor is a great way to ask your partner for your love language to be met. I'm a big believer in teasing and flirting. Just using your voice is a powerful way to express that vulnerability, which can lead to a more powerful connection. But remember, 55% of communication is body language and 38% is tone, and those are two forms of communication we can also absolutely use in becoming more vulnerable. Sometimes vulnerability is shared between two people in a hug, sometimes it is a look, sometimes it is through words, or through sweetening our tone. There is always room for creative expression in leaning into our vulnerability. The trick is to know what sensory responses you deeply cherish and to communicate what those responses are to your partner that make you feel deeply connected and seen.

No one can tell you what your language is; you have to figure it out for yourself. And your love language can change over time.

When Robbie and I were first married, we were so young. I was nineteen and he was twenty-three. At the time, I thought my love language was receiving gifts. I recently decided to retake the test, which you can do with your partner using this link: Love Language Quiz.

My results changed. Touch came out as the top love language for me. (Oh, I still love gifts….) It's good to re-engage in quantifying our needs and what excites us on a regular basis. Even if you take the test today, it may change in the next ten years. You may wind up adapting your needs. When my kids were babies, and I had a newborn, touch was not one of my top needs because I had a baby on me all the time. I was like, "The language of touch? Just buy me perfume!" But as I've gotten older and I began the process of empty nesting, I found myself cherishing nurturing touch.

If someone feels disconnected, and there is little to no intimacy in the relationship, I am convinced that many times it's because one of the love languages is just not being communicated.

As Lauren shared, "A husband once shared with me that he would do acts of service for his wife—for example, he put a glass of water by her bedside, or cleaned up. But that wasn't her love language. She did not interpret that experience as a loving gesture. She didn't even really notice it. It's important that we are aware of how our partners demonstrate love and how our partners receive love.

If it's not in alignment, that's how arguments can come up." The silver lining in quarantine? Couples had a lot more time to practice this method of communication.

For some couples in a post pandemic world, being stuck together for hours on end led to a malaise, and it was difficult to find their way back to one another in creative ways. When restaurants, bars, concerts, and movie theaters were all closed, date night was not exactly exciting. This forced couples to get creative in how they related to one another.

From the interviews I conducted, the pathway to intimacy boiled down to adding play time to the relationship and scheduling romantic dates. For example, Robbie and I decided to take weekly hikes. We surfed LA for the best coffee we could buy, and drank our hot cups of joe by the ocean. We attended Zoom weddings in our living room dressed to the nines. During that time there were plenty of ways to forge connections and to spice up life. All it took was a little bit of "Yes, and...."

CHAPTER 9

NURTURING CHILDREN IN A CHAOTIC WORLD

I was once cast in a TV talk show pilot where I was asked to intervene between a mother and her son on how to repair their relationship. The mom complained that her son was smoking weed, isolating, and being extremely disrespectful. I am a big believer in the idea that children don't ignore their parents, act disrespectfully, or isolate without a reason. Upon probing the son further, he admitted that his father had abandoned him as a child. His mother remarried a man who was emotionally toxic and abusive to him. The son had felt replaced, thrown away, and disregarded by his mother, who was more invested in her relationship with her husband. The son appeared extremely agitated and angry. And the mother was claiming her son's rage, disrespect, and constant rebellion was the root of their family's disharmony.

I asked the mom a pointed question. "When was the last time you and your son spent any quality time together?" To which the mom answered, "Well, I try, but he's not interested." The son looked shattered. I noticed a tear fall down his face. The mom was so caught up in her story, in defending her side, she failed to notice her son. She failed to see his pain. She failed to see his loneliness. I asked the son, "When you get home from school, who is there to greet you?" Her son said, "No one." I asked, "And when you eat dinner, what questions does your mother ask of you?" He responded, "We don't eat dinner together." It was at that moment the son broke down and cried. The mom barely noticed his tears.

I looked at the mom and said, "Your son is not suffering from a case of disrespect. He is suffering from a case of disregard—from you. Get to know your son. Really look at him, prioritize him, only see the good in him, and he will not find the need to recoil from your approach."

The best thing we can do for our children is to look. To really see them and take notice. To support their journey, instead of judging their journey. They will get plenty of judgment from the world. They need their parents to be their safe haven.

It is impossible to write a book on how to forge through a crisis without discussing how to parent during one. Sharon Kaplan Roszia is the ultimate nurturer. She's a social worker, and a leading adoption expert—probably the top one in the world. Sharon was awarded the Humanitarian Award and she's been counseling families for over five decades on how to create safe and loving environments. She entered the field of foster care and adoption in 1963, and has worked consistently in both public and private agencies, as well as private practice, always focusing on child welfare issues. Sharon has lectured extensively all over the United States, as well as Canada and Australia. She's written three books: *The Open Adoption Experience, Cooperative Adoption,* and *The Seven Core Issues in Adoption and Permanency,* the latter of which is considered the Bible to experts in the field of adoption. She's appeared regularly on both local and national television shows over the years, including *The Oprah Winfrey Show.*

I was beyond privileged to have gotten the chance to meet her a few years ago. We just clicked— one mama bear recognizing another, I guess. Sharon lives what she does professionally as a foster parent, adoptive parent, parent by birth, and now intergenerationally with her grandchildren and great-grandchildren. She's the ultimate nurturer. I really wanted her on the show to pick her brain on how we can be better moms and dads, and even how we can be better nurturers to ourselves during chaos.

Life is full of ups and downs, and there will always be crises that may upend our lives unexpectedly. To that end, Sharon's advice can ground us into becoming more aware caregivers no matter what future storm we might need to weather. Notice I didn't say "caretaker" but rather "caregiver." Gary Zukov, author of *The Seat of the Soul,* once corrected me on using that phrasing and it always stuck with me. "A caregiver gives while a caretaker takes. There's a big difference," Gary reiterated to me.

The number one issue Sharon witnessed among parents and children during the pandemic crisis was what she called "bouncing between anxiety and dysregulation." Sharon reminded us that us parents are "the leader of the orchestra. If it's going on for parents, it's going on for their children." Maintaining a sense of safety for our children is key to keeping them regulated when a crisis sets in. During uncertain times, our children need to be reassured.

It is so important to be present to the moment, versus perform in the moment. "We need to give permission to not do, do, do, but be, be, be," Sharon said. Sitting in the discomfort when there is a crisis at hand is not an easy task, but leaning into a *being* mentality versus a *doing* mentality can help parents become more present and set a healthy tone for their children.

When we experience a constant emotional up and down, a malaise can creep in. During the pandemic, for example, when our freedoms were curtailed, creating a massive disruption in our family lifestyle, we lost out on celebrations. Babies born during quarantine lost irreplaceable months of learning from the world around them. The prison sentence felt very overwhelming to parents who had to manage their children's schoolwork, to parents who cared for babies without grandparents to share in the burden, to teens and young adults who wanted to seize the day but had no place to put their energy.

Sharon believes a lot of how we regulate stems from actively tuning into our bodies for the sake of regulating our children's systems as well. Children are very smart. They read our reactions. They can hear our hearts beating fast with anxiety when we hug them, and they can feel our bodies when we are in a state of calm. Our calm, or lack thereof, contributes to our children's sense of wellbeing. Our body language is a dead giveaway that can either create strain, relief, or calm within our children.

"We have to take the time to regulate ourselves, so that we can help regulate our children, or the whole family feels upended twenty-four hours a day."

Sharon suggested that the best way we can nurture ourselves as caregivers is to have a "schedule and a framework every day." Creating ongoing routines fosters a sense of serenity. It also helps to maintain a cohesive direction for the family unit. Whether it's waking up every day at the same hour, maintaining the chores, going outside for walks daily, reading poetry to one another, carving time out to play music and sing or dance—there are many different ways we can maintain a semblance of normalcy during an abnormal life interruption.

If you do have a bout of insomnia, Sharon suggested not to stop the entire day by chilling in the easy chair. "Don't nap off and on. Literally get outside. The most important thing is sunshine and movement."

In other words, don't give in to the malaise. While we might have missed joyful moments and experiences because of a family illness or death or job loss, we can recreate some joy through connecting with our children and using gratitude to measure our day's experience. Sharon believes that *"carving out gratitude time keeps us focused on what's going right versus what's going wrong."*

My husband and I have both worked from home for the past few years, so while we got used to the quarantine togetherness routine, we also got sick of being in a stale rhythm. Because Robbie's health was not at its peak, we chose as a family to stick to a strict quarantine after the initial quarantine so as not to further aggravate his already stressed out heart. The fear was, what if he got Covid-19 on top of having a heart condition? While most of the world was already out of quarantine, we were just getting reacquainted with yet another long jaunt of staying indoors for A SECOND QUARANTINE. Altogether, we did close to eighteen months of strict seclusion during the years of 2020 and 2021. Spicing the week up by creating unexpected experiences led to forming a healthier and more regulated relationship with each other, with ourselves and with our children. To create new memories we walked alongside the ocean together. Well I walked, Robbie sat and watched from the bench. He was too weak to walk alongside me. But I didn't mind. We were in the fresh air experiencing the pace of life in a different form, outside of the hospitals, nurses, and the ongoing IV he was now wearing twenty-four-seven. As a human species, we need expanse like the ocean, and we need new experiences to scintillate the brain. Doing the exact same thing every day does not allow our brains to grow. Feeling locked into a small space for so long, especially living in the city, felt claustrophobic. When I put myself in those expansive environments it was very healing. *"Having little surprise events to shake things up a bit, it moves us out of malaise. It helps our kids to feel a sense of joy and expectation,"* said Sharon.

In the beginning of the first quarantine, before Robbie got sick, my five-year-old nephew would come over every day to do fifteen minutes of yoga with me. We loved our time together, and at the end of our session, we would look into each other's eyes, take deep breaths, and repeat mantras together. Mantras like, "You are powerful, you are healthy, Mommy and Daddy are safe and healthy, and we ask God for a healing for the whole world." These experiences helped my nephew release any tension that had been built up from the early stages of fear the pandemic created. Sharon remarked, *"If we hug our children and their little bodies feel tight, it's what I would call little 'tonic bodies' or 'tight bodies.' We really have to soothe them. Massage their backs and shoulders, and remind them to breathe, because one of the things that we saw during the pandemic is that people weren't breathing. They were holding their breath from tension and fear."*

There is no handbook that comes with leaning into uncertain times such as the kind we have globally experienced. When I was younger, I could go to my parents or even my grandparents during a challenging time, and they could give me examples of how they dealt with those particular trials. But today, there are no living relatives who have already experienced a pandemic. So we are left to use our own intuition to heal, and it begins with self-regulating. Our generation has become more isolated. Technology has forced us to become I-centered. The iPhone and iPad are both examples of this. How ironic is it that Apple's logo is the same fruit two people shared together in the Garden of Eden—the very fruit which isolated them from God and eventually drove them to a deeper spiritual isolation? While we are using these tools to be more connected, we couldn't be further apart. Finding spontaneous ways to connect with our children—without screens—can help our bodies regulate and relieve tension and anxiety.

For every age there are different approaches to parent our children in the middle of uncertainty. Sharon walked us through each age group and gave us real brass-tacks advice for how to support their journeys.

TODDLERS

When explaining uncertainty to our toddlers, Sharon suggested our children are hyper-aware of more than we realize. Toddlers need to be given a sense of safety, certainty, and reassurance, which means lying is off the table. Instead, Sharon suggested we speak directly to our toddlers by saying, *"Things are kind of odd right now.... We're all having to do things to take care of each other...we're in it together, and we are safe and the grownups know how to take care of themselves and we know how to take care of you."*

Of course, in the event our toddlers witness us being frightened by something, like a family member who is hospitalized, or in the event they catch us mourning or crying, Sharon suggested we reassure our children. We can let them know we take notice that they see our emotions, and that it is okay to be sad. *"These are the words I use: 'mad, sad, glad.' We can tell our children, 'It's okay for mom and dad to be mad. We are okay. We won't be mad forever. It's okay for mom and dad to be sad, or even confused. But we're grownups and we know how to do that. And when you're a grownup, you'll know how to do that, too.'"*

TWEENS

When our tweens experience a disruption, it is extremely difficult because they are just beginning to find their individuality. Kids between the ages of ten and fourteen try to discover who they are as independent people. When uncertainty rears its head, and they are still depending on their parents to feel safe while practicing their own independence, that conflict requires extra patience. They're in the age group where they want to know the facts. The best way to support them, Sharon recommended, was to give them those facts. *"Explaining things in a factual, scientific way is the best way to speak to this group."*

This age group is just hitting puberty and have a lot of hormonal shifts happening, which means they need movement. They need to ride their bikes, play tennis, kick a ball, and get some form of routine exercise. *"Let them know this is going to make them feel better because movement releases endorphins. Remember, this is the age group that needs to be out, they need to be active, and they want the facts,"* Sharon shared.

In the event we find our children in either of these age groups having chronic emotional outbursts due to the uncertainty, the best way to support them is to redirect and empathize. Ignoring their feelings by minimizing their hurt can cause even more anxiety and hurt. *"Our kids talk to us with their behaviors. They're telling us something. When our children have an outburst, after they have calmed down, a good conversation starter which will help them to open up might sound something like, 'It seems like you're really frustrated. It seems like you're trying to tell me something. It seems like you're angry.' Whatever it is that you're watching their bodies do, name it. We need to remember that children do what they do because they're trying to tell us something with their behaviors. Our job as parents is to be decoders of our children's behaviors and to recognize that if we're missing the mark, the behaviors go up. If we're on target, the behaviors diminish,"* Sharon reiterated.

TEENS

The big complaint most parents have with their teens is their propensity to isolate in their rooms when they are feeling overwhelmed by fears of the unknown. While they need that privacy, if that is their only experience—especially during a storm—it can lead to anxiety, depression, and a host of emotional misbehaviors.

During quarantine, for example, my teenager was not used to hanging out with mom and dad all the time. In the end, we made it work, and it became a blessing to get to know each other better and to forge a better relationship. Sharon acknowledged that the number one challenge she noticed for teens during lockdown was "They were either sleeping too much, were angry, or were overly agitated."

Our teens rebel because they are supposed to. *"The question kids face when they become teens is, "How do I break away from my family, particularly if I'm a little scared…particularly if I'm not sure whether, if I break away, I will still have my family to come back to…? Our kids are going through a normal stage in an abnormal situation. It is important to be able to say to them, 'These are the parameters. You can be really mad at us. You can say what you want to say. If you want to call me names, say it out loud in your room, just don't let me hear it. That's the only rule here. There are things that you're going to feel. What can we do to help you move through those feelings? Do you need boxing gloves…what do you need? Do you need to go for a run? How are we going to work that tension off?' Talk about what you could do to be helpful, and then figure out ways to tackle that solution together,"* Sharon suggested.

Six months after the initial quarantine began, my teenage son fell and tore his ACL. The night we were in the ICU together, we had a disagreement which led to a heated argument. When we came home from the hospital, I sensed the reality of the altercation lay in his disappointment and helplessness in not being able to surf or run outdoors during an already frustrating time, versus in his disappointment or frustration with me. My initial instinct was to get angry at his disrespectful response. My initial response was to pay attention to my disappointment instead of paying attention to his disappointment. I wasn't proud of how I handled the altercation between us. But afterward, in an effort to mend our argument, I came clean to him about how I mishandled the situation. As parents we are human, and there are times we make mistakes. I think it's imperative that in those moments, we acknowledge those errors if we want to foster closer relationships with our children. As Sharon said, when it comes to parents making mistakes, *We have to forgive ourselves for our lack of perfection. Mistakes are opportunities to teach our children about the do-overs.*

My son deserved that acknowledgement, and he needed me to recognize his disappointment and his frustration. I reached out and he responded with the same compassion. We hugged it out for a while. Sometimes we imagine our teenagers don't need hugs anymore, that they are too cool for school, but they still need touch and they still need warmth. Our love and our touch makes a difference. Mostly, they need to be seen for their full selves. That experience brought us closer.

We decided that because my son would be suffering through a surgery on his knee followed by nine more months of physical therapy during a pandemic, we needed a plan that would offer him a place to relieve his anxiety and his need for movement. We got creative. He took up guitar, I hired my brother to teach him how to play, and we sang together every night. We took a frustrating disappointment and we turned it into a place for creativity and connection. A few years later, when he was adapting to his first year of college and finding it difficult to articulate his emotions, he began writing his own songs. He used music as his pathway to heal and to find ways to express his feelings. Little did I know then, that moving through his ACL surgery recovery using song would serve him later in life as well.

The number one thing Robbie and I have learned as parents is to see the best in our children and to notice their gifts. The world is a difficult place, and there will be plenty of folks willing to see our children with critical eyes. Our children should feel the safest and the most seen by us. Pointing out their deficiencies is not our job. Supporting them unconditionally with love and acceptance is the job. Seeing their gifts and helping them find their heart song is the greatest endowment we can make in our children.

If you are struggling to find healthy ways to react to your children or forge relationships that create trust, love, and healing, ask yourself, "Am I making my child a version of myself that I am trying to correct, or am I seeing my child for her or his full self? Am I taking him or her in with my full acceptance?" Sometimes that shift is what can change a relationship from hostility into compassion. As my brother Yaakov so eloquently put it, "We go from being caregivers when our kids are little to eventually life coaches when they become teenagers and young adults."

YOUNG ADULTS

During the pandemic, the 20-something age group was probably getting the rawest end of the deal. As Sharon so said, *"They had all this independence, they got all this education, they were raring to go, yet there was nowhere to go. They were harnessed…like racehorses waiting for the gate to open and they were stuck there. They were angry and anxious. Or they were totally depressed. We really needed to encourage them to use the time to create new experiences for themselves and for their brains."*

This is the age group which needs to focus on creating connection, creativity, and service even during a crisis. To support their brains into fully developing, which doesn't usually happen until age twenty-seven or twenty-eight, this age group needs new experiences. Sharon suggested that volunteering themselves to be of service is a great solution to calm nerves and promote their own sense of control in an out of control situation. *"They've got to get moving and find ways to be in service so they don't get stuck."* That's true for all of us: we all need to be of service to others in order to find meaning and purpose.

When young adults face a difficult challenge, what helps them move through it is to find creative ways to stay engaged, inspired, and stimulated. In the event we find our young adults isolating or struggling, introducing therapy can be a helpful strategy. The twenty-something age is usually the perfect time for understanding emotional awareness that their teenage brains could not grasp yet. If they can get to know themselves through energy work, talk therapy, or movement, it can be a productive way to engage in their personal growth.

Sharon's ability to honor the challenge we face as parents yet introduce healing strategies for every age group is the ultimate expression of nurturing ourselves and our children. For example, the lockdown offered a silver lining in how we can awaken our nurturing tactics and become better and more present listeners, as we pay closer attention to our children's behaviors. There was a real opportunity to tap into paying attention with our full selves during the quarantine challenge. As Sharon shared, *"We were given an amazing gift to slow down, to pay attention, to prioritize what's important to us and between us and our children."*

The stillness of quarantine allowed us to stay present even among the chaos. In my experience a crisis does not last forever. There are lulls and small moments of reprieve. If we take those moments to surrender to the quiet, it has the capacity to create new connections grounded in healthier and more meaningful interactions between family members. I believe the pandemic, like any crisis, afforded us a new shift. Inside the fold of discomfort a new truth was awakened. It may not be the awakening we want today, but it is the revival we need for tomorrow. And that, I believe, is a truth most parents are deeply grateful for. As Sharon so beautifully challenged us to ask ourselves, *"Do we want to go back to the same old rush, rush, rush runaround? Or do we want to maintain the lessons?"*

PART 3

HEALING YOUR
BODY & SOUL

CHAPTER 10

NURTURING SLEEP
& WELLNESS

How does stress affect our bodies and why does it ruin our sleep? During a crisis, our emotional stress spikes. It can increase depression and insomnia. While Robbie was ill, my anxiety was through the roof. Because I knew his heart was barely pumping, every night I was up checking to see if he was still breathing. "Take an anti-anxiety pill," the doctor said. But they didn't tell me that anti-anxiety pills might cause even more anxiety before they actually started working. I didn't have time to spend adapting. I needed a quick fix so that I could be the caregiver I knew I needed to be for Robbie. After much deliberation, I ditched the pills and chose exercise instead to tackle my nerves. I worked out hard daily and meditated morning and night to help with my moods and my insomnia. We all have to listen to ourselves and our bodies to know what we need when a crisis rages. I've taken antidepressants before, and there have been times in my life when I had no option but to tackle chemical imbalance with preventative medicine. I decided I'd give myself three days. If after three days of working out, eating healthy, and meditating, I still felt unhinged, I would take the pills. But after three days, I was feeling more grounded. Each day I assessed how I was feeling through my journal. I kept myself accountable. I did not want to get to a place of no return.

Dr. Roger McIntyre, a professor of psychiatry and pharmacology at the University of Toronto and head of the Mood Disorders Psychopharmacology Unit at the University Health Network in Toronto, has reported that "In 2020 prescriptions for anti-anxiety medications rose to 34.1% from mid-February to mid-March alone. And the number of prescriptions billed for antidepressants and sleep disorders also increased 18.6% and 14.8%, respectively, just from February 16th, 2020, to March 15th, 2020."

When I turned forty-five, I went to the doctor for a physical. "I am utterly exhausted," I said. "I can't feel my toes. I'm so tired!" To which my doctor responded with sleepy eyes, holding what I'm assuming was his fifth cup of coffee, "So am I, so am I. And not only am I tired, but I would say every single patient that I've seen has had the same exact complaint. They're absolutely exhausted." I asked, "Is there a cure?" And he said, "No. This is adulthood." I couldn't believe it! There was no cure? This is what we signed up for? Just grin and bear it till the grave? "Is that what you're telling me?" I asked the doctor.

"Pretty much..." he said. "But I'll give you a prescription for Trazodone. It'll calm your anxiety and depression, and the best part is that it'll make you sleep like a baby without the grogginess that other sleep aids might give you."

I was pretty happy. A little pill was about to get rid of my moodiness, my carbo loading, my depression, and my anxiety. Sign me up!

Little did I know that this tiny little pill would cause other awful symptoms, like brain fog and losing time. Literally, I didn't know what happened from one hour to the next. I had no clue that my husband had been talking to me. And then later he'd say, "Remember, we had that conversation?" and I couldn't remember it. I had completely lost that time. I forgot words. I forgot appointments. I had short-term memory loss. Yeah, it was that bad. And then I came across an article that changed everything. Written by Locke Hughes, it was entitled, "When It's More Than Just 'Tired:' My Adrenal Fatigue Story."

I had the chance to interview Locke Hughes, a health coach and a journalist who also wrote a book entitled *Melatonin: The Natural Supplement for Better Sleep*. In it, Locke revealed some important details about how we can best nourish our bodies so we sleep better.

1. CBD oil is a non-habit-forming and fantastic sleep aid that does not leave you with brain fog or residual exhaustion like other sleep aids or pharmaceutical drugs often do.
2. Lifting weights is the best way to fortify our bodies. It builds strength and brings oxygen to our muscles, which can keep the fountain of youth really going for years to come.
3. Taking a probiotic to keep your gut healthy is essential.
4. Eating healthier fats and avoiding sugar and alcohol are also musts.

There are a lot of different thoughts on adrenal fatigue. It's a controversial diagnosis. There are some doctors who don't even believe it is real, but others say when our adrenals release the stress hormone, cortisol, we can over-exhaust ourselves. Our bodies are machines, and if they are producing too much cortisol, it can wreak havoc on our system. Lifting weights, jumping, cardio, breathing deeply, going outdoors, and getting sun are all ways we can lower our cortisol levels. Locke described her own adrenal fatigue that felt like, "A fog blanket that comes over you at around three or four p.m. every day." She said that when she got home from work, "I would just fall asleep immediately, wake up at eight, eat, and then go back to sleep."

I related to that a lot. There is no question that our mental stress can affect us physically. Locke had said, "When we're under chronic, long-term stress, our adrenals get fatigued. Hence, the term adrenal fatigue."

Locke also stressed how much our body's function begins in the gut. If our digestion is not functioning well, "It's going to affect all the systems in the body, especially immunity."

In 2019 and 2020 I ran the Miami Half Marathon to help raise money for Rabbi Yitzi Hurwitz, who was suffering with ALS. Yitzi's wife Dina has been a dear friend and sister to me since childhood. It was a no-brainer that I come on board for the fundraiser.

I needed a lot of probing to say yes to a marathon. Most people have it on their bucket list to run a marathon at least once in their lifetime. It was on my bucket list to NEVER run a marathon at any time during my lifetime. But alas, our friend Bracha Lipkind decided to run one year with two friends, and a couple years later she had convinced one hundred runners to do the same—a feat she has managed to rope most of us childhood friends into. I never had a chance to say no. The Run4Yitzi team focused on raising $150,000 toward Rabbi Yitzi's medical expenses.

I am deeply proud of what Bracha accomplished and what I got to be a part of, but it turned out, the stress on my body from my training had contributed to a lot more cortisol exhaustion than I expected. Locke had also trained for a marathon, which led to her adrenal fatigue. I identified very strongly with the worn-out feeling Locke described.

My training for three to six months, with a regimen of running three miles at six each weekday morning and long eight- to ten-mile runs each Sunday had me pooped! Add in a pandemic and job uncertainty, and that is a whole lot of stress to an already fatigued body. I found myself super exhausted those first few months after the pandemic broke out. I was flat on my face. Which brings me to my next discovery about supporting our bodies.

Right after the marathon, which I ran a month before the Pandemic hit, I marched my aching body, after running for three solid hours, into the spa for a massage. I was feeling powerful, strong, and proud of my body, which had weathered this storm of running for so many months. But all of that came to a halt when the massage therapist said to me, "Your muscles appear to be weak. Have you been doing any weight training?" There's nothing like getting up from a massage table and hearing your massage therapist tell you, "You really have no muscle tone. You need to get back into the gym. Have you been working out at all?"

I had just run a freakin' marathon that morning! To which he responded, "You're not doing enough to support your musculoskeletal system. You've got to work out differently."

In my interview with health coach Locke Hughes, she supported the massage therapist's assertion that cardio should not be the only form of exercise we rely on.

"I don't want to say cardio is bad, because it is important for heart health. That's the only way to really train your heart. In the 2000s, there was so much emphasis on cardio—for example, when SoulCycle became really popular and Flywheel—and everybody became cardio bunnies. And there's nothing inherently wrong with that. Some people are built to be ultramarathon runners. But I think, for the majority of us, it can really burn us out. I also think that a lot of women, myself included, thought that maybe yoga would count as strength training, but unfortunately, that's not even enough. I looked good, I felt fit. But I didn't have the muscle, because I was basically just doing yoga with light weights. That's not enough. We need heavier weights at least two days a week. It'll keep your metabolism humming for years in the future."

After supporting your body, nutrition, and sleep, it's time to get holistically aligned—mentally and emotionally. Locke recommended we "do some reflection and learn to figure out what makes you happy and face what is out of alignment in your life." In other words, we need to pay attention, slow down in the quiet, and listen by asking ourselves, "Are we taking the opportunity to finally hear that inner voice?"

A neuro-endocrinologist by the name of Dr. Bruce McEwen, a professor and researcher for the Hatch Laboratory in Rockefeller University, discovered how cortisol actually affects and changes the hippocampus part of the brain. Dr. McEwen discovered that stress hormones leave an impact on our memory and how we react to our recollections. Which means, memories can stress us out and change our brains, and not necessarily for the better. Like the way my husband's heart condition triggered my memory of caring for my father with a similar heart illness, our brain will get a surge of stress which has the potential to shift our thinking from a calm state to a stressed-out unnerving place. The memories cause the stress to emerge, our cortisol gets turned on, and now our stress response is on high alert. It also means, according to Dr. McEwen's research, that the memories that cause our stress are also shifting our brains. We need something to rewire our brains so the stress doesn't morph our wiring and create mental exhaustion.

It makes me wonder if adrenal fatigue was a result of being stuck in a loop of remembering stress, especially when the barrage of news touting death tolls, climate change, and frequent crime sprees seemed to be constantly on repeat. How do we get off that hamster wheel of fear that triggers stress responses? How do we master our brain into a place of constant calm versus constant fight or flight? Can we rewire our brains? The answer is yes. And it involves meditating.

We are all made up of energy. Being still and tapping into our different brain waves using breathwork and meditation can literally rewire our brains and change our thinking mode from a stressed-out state to a calm one. We can become addicted to our stress, our negative emotions, and our obsessive thoughts about the past. And when we connect to the emotions of the past, we live the past every day. Living in the past and worrying about the future does not give us the opportunity to experience the moment. It becomes like an insane *Groundhog Day*. And that, my friends, is what causes severe fatigue.

While our days might be filled with obligations and responsibilities, there's no question that the added stress levels during a crisis can contribute to our emotional unrest. If I've learned one thing from the experts on *The Nurture Series*, it's that we've got to listen to our bodies and nurture ourselves so we can function at our most optimum health. Mindfulness is really the cornerstone of wellness. Check in with yourself. Ask yourself, as Locke Hughes asked of us, "Is what I'm doing today nourishing me or not?"

If our alarming reactions do not nourish us, we shouldn't beat ourselves up over the faulty patterns we have created. We should be patient with ourselves and search for a coach, a friend, or a partner to help keep us accountable.

When it comes to sleep, if there are nights where you find yourself staring at the ceiling at 3 a.m. like I did, because those cortisol levels are out of whack, first of all, text me because I'm probably up. (Just kidding, I'm finally sleeping again!) But secondly, and more importantly, get more information about your health. Get evaluated by your doctor, look into taking CBD oil for a few days to reset your sleep patterns, eat clean, call your therapist, download that meditation app or that strength training app. And lastly, add creativity and sharing with others into your daily routine.

Listen to what your body is telling you. It is the smartest machine, and it will be able to aid your journey by slowly hinting how you can best support your health.

(Also Bracha, I'm coming for you....)

CHAPTER 11

NURTURING OUR INNER SPIRIT

According to Kurt Vonnegut, author of *The Sirens of Titan*, life feels meaningless after experiencing "Empty heroics, low comedy, or pointless deaths." In 2020, the world lost Ruth Bader Ginsburg, ran out of toilet paper, and mourned the loss of 1.83 million. But—is life meaningless? Or is there a collective search this seemingly meaningless experience has sparked within us?

As a human species, we are hardwired to find meaning. Throughout my time as an interviewer on *The Search Series* exploring the meaning of life, I noticed that those who stopped searching for meaning did so out of apathy or despondency. In Victor Frankl's book *Yes to Life* he writes, "Doubt about the meaningfulness of human existence can easily lead to despair."

Life without the search for meaning can lead to anxiety, mental health issues, and in many cases, suicide.

At the end of most of my interviews on *The Nurture Series*, I asked my subjects "How do you nurture your spirit?" Most interviewees took a distinct pause before answering that question. Even though many of the experts I spoke to are deeply spiritual—and in the earlier part of our discussions spoke about meditating, journaling, or even practicing yoga—when asked how they nurture their spirit, they hesitated. Why? What is it about our spirit that eludes us? Furthermore, the interviewees who did not practice ritual regularly would not only pause, they would display embarrassment, unable to answer the question without deeper consideration.

For some, ritual is the source of comfort you have come to rely on to ignite your soul. Many find solace in experiencing spiritual life through communal worship. As a result of the pandemic, when our houses of worship closed, or remained open in a more limited way, ritual was disrupted. Suddenly, those who relied on communal ritual to quench their spirit found themselves at a loss. This vacancy created a fissure in the spiritual system, forcing us to find other creative ways to worship and maintain spiritual practice. Is ritual the ONLY way to tease the spirit out? That disruption made me ask the question: How do we tap into the intangible with a new perspective?"

To get a deeper understanding of how to nurture our spirit in this disrupted time, I interviewed my husband, Rabbi Robbie Tombosky. We discussed spirituality in the most real and down-to-earth way. He was able to succinctly answer how to tap into spirit, how to lean into the discomfort of ritual disruption, and how to access faith after it is tested. And he did it with a warmth and understanding that has made his episode the most popular episode to date.

My husband serves as the rabbi and spiritual leader for the young professionals of Beth Jacob Congregation in Southern California. He is also the founder of Sage Philanthropy Advisors, a company which provides strategic consulting by connecting philanthropists to causes that express their deepest values. With a dual role as rabbi and philanthropic advising consultant, he lives his life with his two feet in both worlds: the communal and the global; the spiritual and the physical.

His work as a philanthropic advisor has taken him into the nonprofit sector among celebrities, NFL athletes, pop stars, and entrepreneurs. He's attended nonprofit events with Beyonce, toured with Billie Eilish, organized television episodes highlighting important causes for NFL players and important figures like the Duke and Duchess, and has even put together conferences in the UN with the likes of Lady Gaga that raised awareness on important impact projects. At the same time, he never fails to make himself available to our family, community, and neighbors. Like our elderly neighbor who calls him day and night to fix her telephone (which isn't really broken). Or Eda, who broke her leg, and recently stopped by to thank me for marrying the man who takes out her garbage every night. (I had never even met Eda before.) Or the seven-foot-tall Russian plumber who stopped by to fix our sink, learned he was Jewish during a conversation with the rabbi, and decided to have a bar mitzvah in our living room with his newfound friend, Rabbi Robbie.

Robbie leads a rich life, filled with tremendous experience in being of service to everyone. He finds his inspiration through learning and connection, through service and introspection. Where I would be more comfortable alone, quietly reading, writing, and meditating, Robbie is an extrovert, most comfortable gathering a crowd with an enthusiasm I deeply admire.

When Robbie was a younger man, he had not even entertained the idea of becoming a rabbi. When he was a child, he carved out a hiding place in his ceiling for the stash of dollar bills he earned working in a local bookstore. Robbie has been employed since the age of twelve. At one point, he was so excited about making money that he would come home, take out his stash from his hiding place, and iron his dollar bills, as though they could lose their value from a wrinkle. As a young man, his goal was to become a lawyer, and to eventually become extremely wealthy. There's nothing wrong with either of those dreams. But he wasn't driven by the idea of changing laws or defending people as much as he was by using materialism to measure his success. A success he believed would provide endless happiness and contentment.

At sixteen, his rebellious spirit proved too much for his high school administration. He became the only student in his class who got a pass for playing hooky. Which meant that every day he left school at noon to attend a gym downtown while the rest of the world thought he was learning about God and faith. At the age of seventeen he met a teacher who positively inspired him to seek his spirit, which has impacted him until this very day.

This teacher had very little material wealth. He had thirteen children, and was very poor. However, every time Robbie visited his home, the man was unspeakably joyful. Robbie once asked his teacher, "Why are you always so happy? You have so little to be happy about…you have so much worry, and constant financial distress. What's your secret?" To which his teacher replied, "The secret to endless happiness can be found in your sense of clarity of purpose. If you know why you are here, you will know how to access the joy even when the pain arrives, because you will be in alignment with your soul's mission."

To Robbie's teacher, accessing joy had nothing to do with material things. It was about cultivating the inner sanctum. The art of never succumbing to despair is focusing on what matters most— which is why Robbie says he became a rabbi. Because what mattered most to him was connecting to others and impacting them with the same enthusiasm he had experienced with his holy teacher.

When I asked him how he nurtures his spirit, he admitted he finds spirituality in the connection with others. When he first became a rabbi, he asked a good family friend, Rabbi Abba Perlmutter, what he felt the job of a rabbi was. To which Abba replied, "The job of a rabbi is to comfort the agitated and to agitate the comfortable."

Robbie often says, upon meeting someone new, that there are three options to be weighed. The first is to determine if you are meeting that person for yourself. The second is to determine if you are meeting that person for that person. And the third is to explore together if that meeting is to help a third party. For Robbie, his spirituality materializes in collaboration. There is so much we can learn from collaboration. We learn how to be from the other person and sometimes we can even learn how not to be. Even toxic relationships can be a springboard for growth. Through every interaction we can learn lessons that awaken our truth and our best selves. "The whole idea of partnership in general, in terms of two people, despite gender, has a powerful connotation in terms of how you can find what's lacking in yourself through another person," Robbie shared. "There's a great story about a group of people that were blindfolded, put in front of an elephant, and asked to reach out and describe the object in front of them. One was holding the tail. One was holding the trunk. One was holding the side. There was not one individual alone that could tell what the animal was or what the entire shape was. But if everybody collaborated and gave their perspective, then they could put the entire picture together," Robbie explained.

I think the elephant can be seen as a metaphor for God as well. God is a difficult entity to understand. He is larger than any thought we can inhabit. But we can gain a perspective of our Higher Power by collaborating together with others to discover the entire shape. We can't learn about ourselves or our Higher Power without that collective consciousness functioning cohesively.

This global crisis brought on a collective consciousness like never before as we all battled to find meaning in the wake of illness, uncertainty, opposing politics, and financial loss. There is a new awareness of how connected we all are. Every microcosmic decision creates a macrocosmic effect. Our actions have a direct impact on one another. Not since 2105 BCE, the year of Noah's flood, has the entire world been affected by a global event simultaneously. And yet we were ironically stuck in our homes, literally washed up on our own small islands, forced to ignite our spirits alone. It was as if God Himself was telling us that our singular actions have significance. To mend the community, we must start with ourselves. But to maintain our spirit, we must not neglect our community. How do we foster community when communal life gets disrupted as it was during the pandemic?

Rabbi Robbie gave us a few concrete ways to revive our spirit in spite of the social divide, the financial strain, the disruption to spiritual communal life, and the health crisis. He explained that to access our spirit we need to "Let go, lean in, love bigger, and live large."

LET GO

One of the great enemies to spiritual growth is holding on to expectations. Holding on to a sense of disappointment from the past that no longer serves this moment will ruin the moment. "Disappointment is honest and real. And we have to process that disappointment. But if we let past experiences, or our expectations, shade and color the moment we are in right now, it's not going to serve us," he said. When our expectations inhibit us from being in the moment, it weakens our spiritual practice. We must let go.

It's important to recognize what we are holding on to that is not serving us. Is it resentment, grief, anger? When we are drowning in an ocean of feelings, exhausted from swimming against the tide, the only way to save ourselves is to surrender to the waves and allow them to carry us to the shore of acceptance. Letting go gives us the opportunity to notice the important goals and the important relationships that we wouldn't otherwise notice.

Letting go creates another advantage. Imagine every difficult emotional event creates a layer, a protective shell, which in some cases feels like a scab. It is there to help you heal. But if the scab does not heal? Then oftentimes this shell, forged to protect, winds up being a barrier blocking you from becoming the new person that you were meant to be. The shell begins to inhibit your growth. When you let go, picture yourself shedding this shell. Walk into a new place with your new body, with your new mindset. Notice how your life can renew itself with this new nakedness without being so guarded. Suddenly you become more open to new ideas, new people, and you can attract higher vibrations and opportunities. If you are using your shell to protect yourself from new experiences, then it is no longer protection, it is the barrier creating your isolation. See what happens when you let go.

LEAN IN

When the High Holidays approached as the pandemic was gearing up, Robbie was dreading going to synagogue. "How do I engage with people from six feet apart, wearing a mask and PPE?" For a man who relies on connection to foster his spirit, this new reality was daunting. But it was also an opportunity that had Robbie rediscovering new ways to connect and lean in. Finding our spirit in a house of worship may have temporarily shifted, but it didn't have to end. Realigning our spiritual expectations is about realizing that we can still maintain a deep connection by looking into one another's eyes, even if we were six feet apart, masked, in an outdoor space. We delivered food and medicine to those in need, and connected face-to-face in virtual calls. We leaned in with our full capacity even when it felt disrupted. There are always creative ways to lean in and forge deeper connections—all it takes is a little bit of will and determination.

LOVE BIGGER

Leaning into these new realities allowed us to love bigger. When we let go of the old and lean into the new with more heart, our spirit soared higher. Loving bigger means we love with our full selves, even our broken selves. Robbie's Uncle Alan lost his first wife, Aunt Judy, when she was only forty-two years old. After the passing of Aunt Judy, Robbie asked his uncle, "How are you able to move through the pain of losing a spouse?" To which Uncle Alan said, "Love bigger." Loving bigger means creating more room in your heart when there is grief, not less. A few years later, Uncle Alan found another love and married Marianne. He walked the walk of loving bigger and it left a wonderful impression on both of us.

LIVE LARGE

Robbie felt the potential reason why people pause when asked directly how they nurture their spirit might lie in shame. We may feel ashamed about not doing enough or not being enough in regard to fostering our faith. Oftentimes we question our own spiritual voice when our sense of self-worth is distorted. The pathway to finding our soul is to live large. If shame is in the way, it is very difficult to lean into our full selves. As Rabbi Robbie put it, "To me, spirituality is very tender, very hard to describe. Spirituality is about being in touch with the best part of yourself. It's about integration and alignment. It's about wholeheartedness in the way you approach life. It's about letting go of shame. And it's about knowing that God loves you the way you are—not in spite of your foibles, but because of them. We're imperfect by design. And if you love yourself, and you can really see yourself through God's eyes, you can begin to have a spiritual experience that is unique to you. I don't think spirituality is something that is abstract and unattainable. I think spirituality is found in the house of worship if you're lucky, but I also think it's found spending time with your loved ones. I think it could be found watching a sunset on the beach. Spirituality is a moment where there's an alignment between our Divine selves and our human emotions, a moment of recognizing the Divine soul that exists. Many of us struggle to be in integrity with our spiritual selves. I think a lot of us carry shame."

Living large is about discovering the self and then leaning in to one's greatness. Robbie shared how important it is to recognize the good leaders in our life, and how they are capable of pointing out our magnificence and revealing our true potential. On the flip side, if we surround ourselves with toxic leaders or toxic friends or family, the opposite holds true. When someone else sees our magnificence, and points it out, we take notice of it. As author Rabbi Jonathan Sacks pointed out in *Morality*, "If I look back at my life, I discover that it was always someone else who set me on a new trajectory... Help, I have found time and time again, comes not from the self, but from others."

Maybe the silver lining to the many crises that have raged globally in the last decade is that the "empty heroics, low comedy, and pointless deaths" have forced us to give in to the discomfort of the not knowing, and to finally explore what we've known all along...that our spirit is a vast universe living inside all of us, waiting to emerge when we let go, lean in, live large, and love bigger.

CHAPTER 12

NURTURING A
FAILED SPIRIT

When we were younger, we may have looked to our leadership—our parents, teachers, and clergy—for the answers. And oftentimes, they were there to be our guide and we relied on them to see our best selves. But I am keenly aware not everyone is that lucky. There are people in positions of power who tear us down instead of lifting us up. Living large becomes living small when corrupt leadership smothers our potential or abuses our inner sanctum. As I told one young man who landed in a Talmudic Seminary in Jerusalem and called to discuss whether it was the right fit for his spiritual journey or not, "To discover if you are in a good spiritual environment, notice how free you feel to be your full self." If you are censoring yourself and unable to lean into your full identity and your full potential, or you're wearing a mask to please others, that's a pretty good indication you are probably not in a good environment with healthy leadership. On the other hand, if you find yourself in an environment where the leadership supports your full self, where you can be a strong expansive critical thinker, then you have landed in the perfect place for growth.

When a spiritual leader has disrupted the spiritual frequency, it can cause catastrophic spiritual shame. Victor Frankl notes that making the decision to survive the German camps by getting in alignment with meaning was unattainable in a vacuum. Despite being reduced to a "nameless thing," he writes in *Say Yes to Life,* there was one pivotal element which kept despondency from taking over: "The critical factor was the existence of others, the being of others, specifically their being role models…." If a leader we rely on devastates us by proving to be a person of no integrity it can feel like an assault on our spirit.

A few years ago, I was invited to be a commentator on the Dr. Phil show. The guest was a young woman named Pearl Reich who said that at the age of seventeen she was married to a man for whom she was clearly unsuited, at her parents' discretion and against her will. Pearl shared claims of "sexual, emotional, and physical abuse by a husband who had never trusted or loved her." Pearl depicted herself as a desperate woman with four young children, trying to escape an abusive and loveless marriage. What made her story ever more scandalous was that Pearl was from a deeply religious Chassidic community. Pearl purported that her husband was so incensed by her decision to become an actress and model that he refused to give her a Jewish or legal divorce. According to Pearl, her husband had threatened to take her children away if she did not abandon her acting and modeling career, a pursuit that he claimed was against the moral values on which they'd based their marriage vows. Pearl was the daughter of a highly influential rabbi from a Chassidic neighborhood. She was deeply wounded that her own father had not come to her defense. Unable to handle the difficult relationships in her life, she chose to flee and take her story public in order to pressure the leaders in her community to help her settle their domestic dispute more fairly. I had never met Pearl before being on camera with her, nor had I been given any details of her story before that day.

Once in the green room, it became apparent that the producers had a specific goal in mind for bringing me onto the show. They wanted to use my voice to question Pearl's decision to live a double life by abandoning her faith in private while pretending to continue her spiritual practice around her family in order to keep up appearances. They were hoping I would point out her hypocrisy, and possibly even become angered by her decision to use semi-naked pictures as an act of defiance. Essentially, I was intended as a pawn to further Pearl's suffering, to discount her story. Hello, daytime drama!

What the hell had I gotten myself into? That's exactly what I kept asking myself as I sipped on my lemon tea while they fluffed my hair and touched up my lipstick in the green room. "Remember," the producer said before seating me in front of the cameras, "you are incensed and enraged by Pearl's immodest and immature behavior."

Daytime TV had written the script, and I was walking right into it. When they gave me my cue, I thought about running out of the room or hiding. But the lights were up—it was too damn late.

There was a woman sitting next to me. She whispered in my ear, "Dear Jesus, this poor girl, you can tell she has completely lost it, poor thing." I'm pretty in tune with people, and I could tell some of the audience was judging Pearl's behavior as erratic and slightly unhinged. Suffering with deep-rooted pain and frustration with her community, Pearl displayed her sexuality in revealing photos. Her tough exterior and defiant approach caused others to see her as unsympathetic.

Dr. Phil's questioning led the audience to assume she might have been putting her relationship with her boyfriend, also onstage, ahead of her relationship with her own children. As a mother, I was triggered. As the daughter of divorced parents, I was very triggered. My reaction could have been pretty incensed, and I might have been applauded.

Pearl was on national television now, she was finally getting the attention she'd hoped to achieve. She was finally being seen. Only, no one was actually looking at her. They were seeing her half-naked pictures, her bleached blonde hair, and her rage. They were not really seeing Pearl.

But I saw something else. I was looking straight at Pearl's broken heart.

Finally Dr. Phil lead in with my prompt,

"Chava is an Orthodox Jewish mother, and she says that she's concerned that Pearl is acting one way in front of her kids and another way behind their backs. Chava, what do you have to say about this?"

As the daughter of divorced parents I knew there are always three sides to every story: her story, his story, and the truth. I knew we were only getting half the story that day, as her ex was not there to defend himself. None of that really mattered, because even if the story was utterly false, I had still made my decision on how I wanted to respond. I turned to Pearl and I looked deeply into her eyes. I connected with her on a soul level and I said,

"You're obviously feeling a tremendous amount of pain. As an Orthodox Jewish woman, I want to tell you, I'm here for you. You're in my heart."

The room became still. As if time and space had converged into a loving hug. For the first time during the entire episode, Pearl choked up. The tough exterior she had fashioned onstage cracked slightly open. There was no longer a reason to behave defensively.

Loving bigger means holding space. Which is why, according to Jewish law, while visiting a mourner, the visitor is not supposed to speak until the mourner has initiated the conversation first. Because the job of the visitor is to hold space. Loving bigger means holding space in one's spirit for the dignity which every person deserves. When a person's spirit has been crushed, the darkest thing one can do is damage it further with flippant judgment. TV producers had written the script, but I refused to buy into it.

In that moment, Pearl and I were both orbiting on the same loving planet without the distractions of the TV cameras or the judgmental audience. We were two souls connecting with authentic understanding.

With so many watching *Unorthodox* on Netflix during quarantine, the conversation I had on the Dr. Phil show eight years ago remains as relevant as ever. Accessing spirit when our faith has been shattered by corrupted role models or community leaders is one of the hardest things to do. That kind of betrayal can choke our spirit in ways that can take years to correct. After the show aired, many abuse victims from the Orthodox Jewish world began talking more openly about their stories. In some ways, this episode opened up the can of worms the Orthodox Jewish world needed to face in order to begin to repair the dysfunction that existed in the shadows. A healing took place.

My goal that day was not to contribute to the drama of daytime television. Rather, it was to be the loving voice in Pearl's head. I had hoped that after everything, while I could not mend her story, I could contribute to mending her heart. Awakening spirit happens when we have positive voices in our head to lean on. It's important to take note of who we surround ourselves with and what voices we allow to inhabit in our minds.

As Robbic suggested, "Ask yourself, do those voices belong there? Have they earned the right to have that place in my psyche? If they don't, then I would invite you to curate some new people in your world, and to surround yourself with some really wonderful spiritual mentors, and people that can help you get to that positive magnificent place. It starts with acceptance, and authentic engagement, putting bias and agendas aside, and allowing ourselves, and those around us, to truly engage, to truly think, to truly be. There is a magnificence in each one of us. We just have to allow that to percolate. Reach out to people. There's no one answer. I think it's very personalized. And I think it's a journey that's worth taking."

When others fail to prove their values by example, we become deeply disappointed. As my father used to tell me, "Place principles above personalities." Because personalities will sometimes let you down, but principles are steadfast.

After you have found that spiritual leader or your spiritual tribe of healthy voices, essentially the job of creating a relationship with your Higher Power is still an inside job. While a leader can inspire you to know where to look, it is up to each of us to actually be open to see God with our full spectrum of spiritual and physical sensations on our own. Oftentimes, we get caught up in thinking

God is a separate entity, when really He is part of each creature. When we see ourselves as separate from our Divine spirit, we have a difficult time answering the question on a podcast show, "How do you nurture your spirit?" God—a word that feels so distant from our own reality—can make it feel like spirituality is an elusive conquest that only a few are destined to master. I once heard the word God referred to as perceptible reality—our reality. We are a piece of that greater reality that exists—even if there are times when we want to run and hide from it.

"We are all composed of two souls: the animalistic soul and the Godly soul. Our heart is divided. When we serve God with our whole heart, we use both sides of ourselves. If I were to use modern-day language, I think when we say Godly soul, that is our altruistic selves. While our materialistic soul is composed of our narcissistic selves," Robbie said.

We have the powerful, imaginative ability to shift our reality using our altruistic voice versus our narcissistic tendencies. Unlike animals, who engage on instinct, humans have the capacity to engage using imagination. When we imagine who we can become or what we can accomplish, it means our spirit is awake. When our imagination is dead, and doubt and despair seep in, our spirit is asleep. In some ways, the most spiritual moment of the day exists at the moment we open our eyes in the morning and set our intentions.

While at a fundraiser a few years ago, Robbie happened to lock eyes with Josh Malina, a veteran actor who has appeared on *West Wing*, *Scandal*, and *A Few Good Men*.

"Rabbi," Malina said to Robbie, "I want you to know, I'm a very proud Jew."

To which Robbie asked, "Wow. What does that mean that you're a proud Jew?"

"It means I teach my kids to be proud Jews."

"How do you teach your kids to be proud Jews?"

Malina's answer was one of inspirational ingenuity.

"Every morning, when Jewish people wake up, we say a prayer. And that prayer is called the Modeh Ani, which translates to mean, 'I give thanks before you, King, living and eternal, for You have returned within me my soul with compassion; abundant is Your faithfulness!' We thank God for giving back our soul. And at the end of the praise we say, 'How great is your faithfulness in us.'"

So which is it? Is spirituality about having faith in God, or in knowing that God has faith in us?

Robbie explained, "Having faith is a fantastic thing. But it can also be a cop out, because instead of taking action, we just leave it out there for some other worldly entity to inhabit. But in truth, what we're saying in that prayer in the morning is deeply spiritual. We've just woken up. Our eyes are barely open. We haven't even put our feet on the floor. And we say, 'God has faith in me. God has given me life.' It's very Brené Brown-esque. It gives us permission to approach our day with wholeheartedness. We are proclaiming in that prayer that we are enough. Being spiritual is knowing that whatever comes our way, we have the capacity and the ability to take it on. And we can engage with that in the day ahead."

During the moments we choose to operate on a soul level—when we are deeply connected to our source, to the slice of this infinite Godly energy that inhabits us—we perform as our supremely altruistic selves. That is when our reality has the potential to morph. Just as Victor Frankl managed to morph his suffering state in the concentration camp. "Existence—to the nakedness and rawness of which the human being was returned—is nothing other than a decision," Frankl wrote in his book *Say Yes to Life.*

We can choose a suffering state or an enlightened one. When we operate from the finite self, we become constrained—we reflect nothing. Like a voice that drops out of pitch, dangling in midair with nowhere to hide its broken song; stuck, stranded, and disabled. When we can't see far, and we have no depth...that's precisely when the pain comes. The pain we create because we won't look deeper, further, wider. The mirror lies face down, yet all we must do is tilt it back up and face the reflection, face the truth. All we must do is accept what we refuse to see but already know—which is that we are a reflection of a Higher Power. That Power is embedded in our existence to let us know we can acquire an infinite view of possibility, an infinite aspect of genuine truth, which shapes our lives and brings color to the black and white picture we might have bought into.

When we lift that mirror up and we finally see ourselves past ourselves—as infinite creatures, all deeply connected—that's when we don't just elevate the world, we literally create a new one. Like the world Pearl and I got to create on national television in that small moment. A world where she saw me, and I saw her. A world where judgment and defensiveness was suspended, where love was the only emotion, and where healing began.

Any time we experience awe it is because we are noticing the duality of north and south, otherwise known as body and spirit, dancing on the battle line at the same time. Together yet staggered. The composition of body and spirit dancing together are like notes pounding the inner ear which allows us to hear our spiritual calling. It is a whisper most days, which we long to know but are oftentimes afraid to acknowledge. Which is why we were so inspired when we heard the united voices sing together during the lockdown from their apartments throughout the world. It's why we were in awe when we heard the collective clapping in Manhattan for the healthcare workers each evening at seven p.m. These harmonized expressions had us in awe and wonder because they were filled with that mystical energy of unifying the physical with the spiritual cohesively. There's a reason why TIKTOK became a $75 Billion company with 450 million users. Because the world wanted to orbit on the grid of joyful musical and humorous cohesiveness. It's why men and women took to the streets in solidarity to confront racism, chanting in unison "Black Lives Matter." Because we long to express our altruism together, and to express our joy, our pain, and our collective spirit together.

According to the Zohar, our world is referred to as "the world of action." We are bound by space, time, and matter. We are not just bound by ideas, we are also bound by the pen that inscribes the prose. Spirituality cannot exist by contemplation alone. It needs something actionable to hold it down in this world. The search for meaning is the very cornerstone on which our spirit relies. If lifting weights strengthens our muscles, then searching for the meaning of life strengthens our spirit. Searching is the spiritual workout, the actionable conquest. It is where corporeal needs end and the transcendent urge begins. Without searching for spiritual practice into our lives, we are at risk of not having one. And even if we have less than optimal leadership, committing to that inner search and quest morphs us into the leaders we have the potential to become—the audacity to assert, the ability to command. Who knows, you might just become the champion pointing the compass north, which someone else needs to find on their own shaky life voyage.

PART 4

HEALING AND THE ART OF SURRENDER

CHAPTER 13

NURTURING GRIEF & FAITH

The year 2020 began with a lot of hope and promise for me. I had been cast in two television series for Warner Brothers. I was about to embark on an incredible adventure as a talk show host, and I had just wrapped on a year-long endeavor working on a documentary. A comedic television show I co-wrote and co-starred in had just been screened in two film festivals and had been awarded Best Series. I was excited to start pitching that as well as another fully developed show I had just finished writing with my writing partner. AND I had just finished running the Miami Half Marathon for a fundraiser which helped raise $150,000…way more than we had expected to accomplish! 2020 promised to be a year of greatness.

Then Covid-19 happened.

From the outside it appeared my life was on a drastic trajectory UPWARD. And in many ways, it was. But the pandemic had other ideas in mind. When the quarantine hit, everything changed. The TV shows I was attached to were canceled, I had to put the pitching on hold for the comedic projects that we had spent two years creating, and suddenly I had zero prospects in front of me. Everything I had been working toward fell into a silence.

The week the quarantine began, the first week of March 2020, was, ironically, my birthday weekend. "Happy birthday!" was the last thing I wanted to hear. I did not feel like celebrating at all. Outside of the looming pandemic, I was also deeply struggling with a lot of unresolved grief that not only included the recent career setbacks, but other personal emotional losses as well. I really believed I had resolved some of these, but it became clear that I'd used my career to ignore them. Once my career came to a halt, I was left staring at the hole of grief slowly eroding my insides. Grief, which had managed to wedge itself inside the recesses of my body for over ten years. There were clues: the constant insomnia, the bouts of depression, the sheer exhaustion that had settled into my bones. But I was really good at masking my disappointment, and had settled into a routine of avoidance and distraction. Then the pandemic hit, and all distractions were GONE. I had no choice but to finally resign myself to nurturing the grief.

There were a few reasons for this grief. One of the biggest reasons was that I missed my children terribly. My eldest son was living in

New York and working for a media company. My daughter was studying abroad. I was getting ready to empty my nest for the third and final time as my youngest was entering his senior year. All I could think of was, "If I'm not mothering, and my career is shit, then what the hell am I going to do? What the hell am I good for?"

The second reason my grief was in full flair-up mode was that I had only recently finished working on a documentary that took me down a rabbit hole of emotions I wasn't really prepared to face. I believed with all of my heart that I had already faced and dealt with the grief of losing my dad, and I didn't have to revisit it again. And yet, there it was, revisiting me like a bad dream. Because apparently grief does not have an expiration date.

The documentary project I worked on highlighted the story of a woman who went on a journey to get to know her mother. She'd been just fourteen months old when her mother died from cancer at the tender age of twenty-nine. On the night of her mother's cancer diagnosis, her mother's father was murdered. For one whole year, I was consumed by a story that dealt with a lot of intense and profound elements of loss, some of which I had experienced in my own life. In order to be a really great storyteller, and an even better director and editor, I could not just watch the story; I had to experience the story so that the emotionality was authentic and genuine. As a director and editor, I found myself telling a story of loss and of victory. Which meant I found myself living and reliving loss every single day for almost an entire year in the editing room. The deeper I got into the storytelling process, the more I began to recognize the grief of losing my father so suddenly over ten years prior still felt unresolved. Coupled with empty nesting, my grief took a dark turn. The same summer I wrapped with the documentary (a few months before the pandemic began), I found myself nurturing my mother back to emotional wellbeing after she experienced the loss of her third husband. (My parents had been divorced several years prior to that.) By the time the pandemic hit, even before my career tanked, I was already battling a storm of emotions. At that point, I figured I could ignore that storm because my career was scoring such big points. And then in a matter of weeks I was left with nothing but my grief for comfort. Not the best comfort, I might add.

Sensing my inner tempest brewing, Robbie realized I needed a pick-me-up. By the time my birthday rolled around, and the pandemic started, I hadn't seen my eldest son or my daughter for many months. I was in a serious funk. One day I walked into the house to find a huge box on our living room floor. It was at least 4 foot by 4 foot. *"Chava, I got you a present!"* said Robbie. All I could think was, *"Oh no, Robbie, what did you do…? I don't need another large kitchen appliance!"* I slowly and methodically ripped off the wrapping paper and as soon as I got the box open, out flew my daughter! She had flown in from overseas to surprise me for my birthday weekend. Then the door swung open and it was my son from New York. We cried and laughed and I hugged everyone so tightly. All we kept saying was, *"At least we have the weekend."*

Then quarantine was announced. We never thought the "weekend" would last for eight months!

As the pandemic swept through our cities I kept thinking about what I could do with my limited resources. I could teach. I could deliver food to those who were elderly or immunocompromised. I could call every person I knew who had lost work, or who was sick, or who might need help paying bills. I could coordinate an effort to ask others to donate toward helping the needy and the sick. I could go shopping and deliver food to those who were strapped for cash. There was actually so much that was in my control. Within a few weeks, my husband and I had used our resources to create Zoom workshops and Zoom meetings so our congregants wouldn't feel so lonely.

We went into action because if there's one thing we really do well, it is tackle crisis. Between the two of us, we had given over fifty classes in that short amount of time, and had delivered hundreds of meals. We had also helped out a few neighbors along the way we didn't even know before the pandemic. Neighbors like Elizabeth, a holocaust survivor who hadn't left her home for two weeks and who had run out of food. Elizabeth had no idea what was happening and had said she hadn't been that scared since World War II.

And although I became really busy volunteering for my community, still, the grief I had been holding in my body was beginning to rumble. It was on a mission to disrupt my relationship with myself. But mostly, it was on a mission to disrupt my relationships with my kids and my husband. It took no prisoners. I began fighting with everyone in the house. My mood swings kept everyone at bay. I had to get this thing under control. You know the saying, *"Happy wife, happy life?"* Well, it's damn true. I was not happy, and I was making everyone else around me pretty miserable. I needed to start implementing some nurturing techniques.

I was tackling the community crisis. That was a great distraction from focusing on my own. Essentially, I was distracting instead of disrupting my patterns. It was easy to help others. The hardest thing for me was to help myself. I really needed to get into therapy. I had to deal with all my unresolved grief. I needed to start taking better care of my body and my mind and my moods. How on earth could I be there for everyone else if I was falling apart at the seams? The question was, how would I pay for the therapy if I didn't have any income coming in because of the pandemic? Here's the thing about the Universe…when you ask it for help, it really does deliver. And then it just sort of happened. I got a call I never saw coming: the Synagogue decided they wanted to give me a small token of their appreciation for all of the classes I had been giving. It was just enough to pay for my therapy. And that's how I put myself back together again. Being of service to others had literally saved me. Let me just say, it is NOT enough to only do for others, because that can also be a crutch. Being there for others was not meant to replace my process of tackling my inner demons.

It was only a means to get me to that next step. If I'd never hit step two, and only consumed myself with being of service to others, that would have been a classic co-dependent situation. I would still be stuck in my grief.

The biggest revelation I learned in therapy, in moving through my grief, was that in order to allow the grief to leave, I first had to give it a seat at my table. I could not ignore it. I could not distract myself by mindlessly watching *Scandal*, by self-sabotaging my personal health through artisan bread and ice cream, or by jumping into a new project to reboot my career. I had to allow myself to feel all the loss. I had to make room for some serious quiet and introspection.

What I found myself doing quite often, every time I felt a hint of grief coming on over this last decade, was very systematic. Here was my mechanism (pay close attention, because I'm really quite proud of how well I managed to mask the problem). Every single time I began to feel helpless or disappointed, normal reactions to my grief, I would criticize myself instead. I had literally learned to trigger that critical voice every single time I began to feel the suffering. That critical voice became my mechanism, which in turn kept me prisoner to the grief and the uncomfortable feelings that Dr. Joan Rosenberg spoke about. I became excellent at pretending and avoiding and using myself as a punching bag to avoid feeling the real pain.

The moment I realized this inner critic was in charge was the moment I realized I could dethrone her. Although my grief needed to have a seat at my table, my inner critic did not deserve to be there. I needed to sit with the grief and allow it to do its thing. Allowing it to flow was a gift I needed to give myself. I needed to feel all of it. I needed to cry and feel it deeply so I could finally bid it farewell. I couldn't distract it away any longer. Grief does not leave a person forever, but I knew I could get to a place where I could manage it without it managing me, I just had to be less afraid to walk into the grief hole. Fear is its own beautiful gift. It can be used to hurt, to save, to control or to protect. Instead of using fear as my bodyguard, I weaponized it to self-sabotage my growth. Avoidance was my armor. Here's a little trick about fear. If you're using it to protect yourself, it is justified. But if you're using fear to hide from yourself, it is hijacking your existence.

In the Biblical text referred to as Numbers, in the portion called Chukat, after the Jews were rescued from their Egyptian enslavement and were wandering in the desert, they complained against God and Moses, saying,

"Why did you make us leave Egypt to die in the wilderness? There is no bread and no water, and we have come to loathe this miserable food."

As punishment for their lack of faith in their Higher Power, The Torah verse continues by saying,

"God sent poisonous snakes to the people. They bit the people and many of the Israelites died."

The remedy? God said to Moses, "Make a seraph figure and mount it on a standard. And anyone who was bitten who then looks at it shall recover."

So Moses fashioned a copper snake wrapped around a pole and every person that stared at the copper snake became healed.

What is this odd story?

The medieval Sephardic Jewish philosopher known as Maimonides explains that this event demonstrated our pathway to healing—which is to use the disease as the cure. In fact, many vaccines work by taking a droplet of the disease which is inoculated as the remedy. By allowing the body to handle the bacteria in small doses, it learns how to effectively cure itself by understanding the chemical makeup of the disease, and building an immunity to combat the illness. In this case, the remedy to the snake bite was to stare at the snake. Inoculating the disease with the disease became the antidote.

Which means, if the body can heal itself with diseases, aren't we capable of healing our emotional trauma using the same uncomfortable emotions as the remedy as well, just as Dr. Joan Rosenberg suggested?

Just like God told Moses to stare at the snake, Dr. Joan encourages us to lean in to the discomfort and stare at the emotion. When we allow our bodies to experience the uncomfortable emotion instead of ignoring the feeling, we become more resilient. We rectify our perceptions, reactions, and impulses and restore ourselves to a place of healing. In other words, by inoculating ourselves with giving ourselves permission to feel the emotion, we counteract the punishment of becoming crippled by the emotion. Instead, we heal the emotion by feeling it. It was high time I felt the grief. It was time to stop allowing the critical voice to be in charge.

That critical voice had me falsely believing it was there for my protection. It wasn't. I was not this critical voice. She was not me. I alone created her, and I alone had the power to deconstruct her. While I had felt that voice was justified, and even felt deserving of her at times, she needed to go. The critical voice had not been my safety net at all; it had been the scam created to blind me from my authenticity. It had been my smokescreen. Blaming others for my feelings of unworthiness, self-shaming, acting and staying small—those mechanisms were put into place by ME. They did NOT SERVE ME. And they could be just as easily ERASED BY ME.

Every person has two life forces pulsing inside their bodies, and each one has a voice. There's the real voice, which tends to get drowned out, and then there's the critical voice, which loves to be both loud and bossy. Both voices consistently compete for airtime in our heads. Some call them consciousness and subconsciousness. Others call them the good inclination and the bad inclination.

Either way, the voices are on play All. The. Time. The key is to know which one to listen to.

The critical voice will spend all its energy sabotaging the real voice, all while convincing you that it is protecting you. It is so good at this, your mind even manages to rewire itself to believe that the critical voice is the actual you. Usually, the morph starts slowly and stealthily. One day it gets so loud that we begin to believe we are that voice. I thought I was that voice. It haunted me like my own shadow, and became excellent at camouflaging my truth and hiding in the shade. When I least expected it, it would get to work. And anytime grief was triggered, the feelings of discomfort would become so enormous that I'd fall apart and the critical voice would take over. The key was to realize that the critical voice was me— but also not me. It was my mask. I could wear it, but I could also take it off. I had to learn to get comfortable feeling uncomfortable.

The question I had to ask was: who was my real voice? What did she stand for, what did she believe? Would I like her without the grief to comfort her? See, to let go of grief, you have to make room for something else. That something else was scary. I had gotten so used to using grief as my companion, I forgot I could find a place where it could coexist without it becoming my partner in crime. But first, I had to find out if I could press mute on that critical voice. It was loud, and it sabotaged my willingness to feel all the frustration, embarrassment, grief, and helplessness I experienced over ten years as a result of my parents' divorce, my father's untimely death, my empty nesting, and the secondary infertility I'd fought through for so many years.

While I knew my grief was not going to go away overnight, I did finally give myself permission to stare at it, welcome it in, and lean into the discomfort. The healing finally began. The healing is still happening! It might continue for a long time, but I am finally okay with all of it.

Shutting the inner critic down and allowing grief in can be terrifying…but it is the only way to awaken into honest freedom. When you can operate authentically from that real voice—at all costs, at all times—that's when everything changes. That's when blessings rain down. When that authentic voice is the only voice we let in, the only voice we listen to, we *slay* life. That's when the real living begins.

That inner critic which had tormented me for so long? I stopped listening to her. I faced my grief and allowed my discomfort to settle into my body. I was done ignoring it by distracting myself.

This is the work I will probably spend the rest of my life practicing over and over again.

Like the snake bite, which only healed after staring at the copper snake, I had to learn how to be courageous and breathe in the poison. And eventually it became the remedy to healing my trauma.

If quarantine has taught all of us anything about forging through a crisis, it is that being still and present is the only way to weather the storm of uncertainty. Nexting and worrying about what's to come only creates more anxiety. I have always leaned in to creativity to save my psyche. But if my psyche is at a breaking point, then creativity cannot thrive. The greatest gift I have given my creativity is to be still. I am finally allowing the aha! moments to come, because I have taken the time to revisit those painful emotions. I am happy to say that creativity finally graced me again. *The Nurture Series* would never have been born, or this book written, without that reboot. I was able to come to terms with my empty nest with grace and joy. I was able to face my personal losses with way more acceptance. I was able to start dreaming again. I was able to make everything okay. I had done the work. I was strong—right?

Wrong. Oh so wrong. Because while my husband's septic condition looked to be healing, there was still a long road we never saw coming to get his heart strong (and apparently an even longer road to get my own shit into gear). His condition was way more uncertain than we expected. There were still so many unanswered questions. Would he need invasive or non-invasive surgery? Would he need a stent in several years because of his 60- 70% blockage? Would he need bypass surgery? There were still so many unknowns.

And then, after six weeks of my husband taking a serious regimen of IV antibiotics twenty-four/seven, we learned he needed open heart surgery to fix his mitral valve, which had completely deteriorated and needed to be replaced. The kicker? I was not allowed at the hospital due to COVID restrictions. Hello grief my old friend once again. Because again, grief does not have an expiration date. But at least this time, I had a few more tools in my toolbox for tackling this matzah ball.

EXERCISE

In my masterclass, "The Expanse Effect," where I teach emotional resilience using meditation and breathwork, I've taken Dr. Joan Rosenberg's approach in allowing the body to reset itself through moving through the uncomfortable emotions using transcendental inhalation and exhalation as a modality to regenerate the mind.

Here is how the meditation, inspired by the Rosenberg Reset, works. I call it SPBS, which stands for Seek, Peek, Breathe, and Speak:

Find a place and make yourself comfortable away from any distractions. Go inside your mind's eye and search for which one of your uncomfortable emotions might be coming up. Remember, according to Joan Rosenberg there are eight and they are: **Sadness, Shame, Helplessness, Anger, Vulnerability, Embarrassment, Disappointment, and Frustration.**

Next, peek into your body's system and then ask yourself which of the eight emotions you might be feeling. Finally, BREATHE. Look at the discomfort directly in the face. Allow your body to feel the emotion and notice where it is taking up space in the body. Do you have pain? Notice where it is residing. Then allow yourself to breathe through that uncomfortable experience for at least 90 seconds. Lastly, speak it through with a friend or in a journal. Get it completely out of your body. By naming it, feeling it and breathing through it, you can finally allow the emotion to stop taking up space.

CHAPTER 14

THE CASE OF THE "WHAT-IS" VERSUS THE "WHAT-IFS"

Every single day that Robbie was in the hospital while we were in Las Vegas, my best friend Nomi called to see how I was doing. In fact, she was the very first call that I made when I heard his diagnosis might be leukemia. On one of our daily calls, Nomi was frantic. Her Aunt Itty and Uncle Tzvi had been buried in the rubble of the Miami building collapse in Surfside. Although the world had opened up on June 15th, 2021, after a long pandemic journey, it still felt like everyone I cared about had their world collapsing.

The daunting reality of my husband's ongoing and unpredictable condition had me reeling. My nights became like trying to drink a glass of ginger ale during airplane turbulence—lots of tossing and turning with zero reprieve from the tension. I would stare at the night sky, flip to the ticking clock, and force my breath into my lungs, while making sure Robbie's fading body was still breathing. It felt like I was holding up a car over my head. As my friend Devorah Leah said to me, "When you are depressed, you are thinking about yesterday. But when you have anxiety, you are fearful of tomorrow." I was locked in a trap of being in tomorrow. The *what-ifs* kept creeping into my mind until my sister Tova said to me, "You're living in the past and you're living in the future, but you're not living in today."

To combat the *what-ifs*, I decided to do three things. During times where my racing mind had the audacity to steal my precious minutes, I experimented by leaning into gratitude, prayer, and healing.

GRATITUDE

While Robbie was having his first heart procedure back in Las Vegas, I wound up in the gift shop and bought a card for Dr. G, who was the ER doctor that saved Robbie's life. Dr. G was a pretty macho guy. He sort of looked like a cross between Batman and a character from Grey's Anatomy. He was kind, but also a bit hardened by seeing sick people daily. "Dr. G, I just want to thank you for everything you did for my husband. I know you pulled a lot of strings to get him admitted. And I just want you to know, if you ever need anything, anything at all, my husband and I will be there for you unconditionally as your rabbi and rebbetzin." I wasn't really prepared for what Dr. G said next. His tough exterior melted. Tears came to his eyes and he said, "Actually, I can't tell you how much I need that right now." There was no way we went to the Las Vegas hospital by chance. I knew that the second I saw Dr. G take my card. There was gratitude in knowing there was purpose to us being there and that stayed with me when I hugged my husband before sending him off for his open-heart surgery. There was a reason for this circumstance and that made it more bearable.

On the night that Nomi's Aunt Itty and Uncle Tzvi were finally found, she called me. And between her tears, she shared stories about her aunt's resilience, and her lovable personality. How her aunt had to say "I love you," to her friends each night before she went to sleep…a tradition Nomi and I have now started. Although I had never had the good fortune to meet Itty and Tzvi Ainsworth, the one thing Nomi kept telling me over and over about her Aunt Itty for all these years was that she had this unshakeable positive nature. "You could be on a tormenting car ride, stuck in the worst traffic, and Aunt Itty would say, "I know we're going to be terribly late, but look how lucky we are that we get more time to be together to chat." Or she could be ill and unable to go to a wedding, and she'd say, "I can't go to a beautiful wedding, but look how lucky I am to be able to watch it from the comfort of my wonderful bed on a Zoom call."

In other words, Nomi's Aunt Itty never for one second felt sorry for herself. She saw the beauty and the wonder in every moment she was alive, even though she contended with an ongoing autoimmune disease that kept her bedridden a lot of the time. Her aunt and uncle were buried together nearly two weeks after the building collapse.

Three days after we finally got home from Vegas, (on our white-knuckle, four-hour drive that ensured my husband was home in time for his next life-saving dose of antibiotics), my son Meir fell ill with a potentially life-threatening condition called rhabdomyolysis. If he had not been wise enough to go to Urgent Care at eleven o'clock that night, his kidneys would have shut down permanently. Once again, I found myself in the ER until six in the morning, sitting in a chair. But this time, it was with my son—only three days after my husband had come home from a two-week stretch in the hospital. I can honestly say that although my son made a full recovery after being in the hospital for four days, I completely fell apart. I felt like I was standing at the edge of a cliff, and when Meir was hospitalized, that was God just pushing me off into the abyss. I think when you're feeling against a wall and diminished the only thing left to do is to surrender. So that's exactly what I did. I allowed myself to stay in bed for one week. And on the seventh day, it became apparent that I was sinking into the *what-ifs* versus leaning into the *what is*.

After some time, rest, and a shift in perspective, I realized I had to summon a little bit of Aunt Itty. I began to make a list of *what was*, so that I could take a break from concentrating on the *what-ifs*. The day I made this list, I started with the small stuff. Like how I had gotten to spend that morning with my husband. How

I got to share a delicious coffee with him. How I finally got to see my best friend, Nomi, and give her a big hug. How I got to have my favorite BBQ pizza from Pizza Nosh with my kids. No one died *that* day. No one was hospitalized *that* day. Overall it was a pretty great day. Were we dealing with a long series of setbacks without an expiration date to the madness? Yes. But I also knew that God was in control of all of it. And He would decide when this troubling time would be over—not me.

My job in all of it was to show up to it with a lot of humor and compassion. I decided to make the choice to lean into all the love I got to be surrounded by with my full heart. I decided to concentrate on how proud I was of my children versus how sad I was that they were about to leave for college and empty the nest again. I was going to change my perspective and see my accomplishments as a damn great mother and wife versus the *I didn't get to yet* or *I didn't accomplish yet*. I decided I was going to try every day to be the best mom and wife I knew how to be so that one day I would look back at this challenging time and we would say, "Wow, that was absurd but not impossible." It was the least I could do to honor the life of my best friend's Aunt Itty. You know the saying, what happens in Vegas stays in Vegas? I decided that no matter what the outcome of my husband's condition, the pain and suffering and fear would have to stay in Vegas. The love, laughter and will would travel with me instead. At least, that's what my intention was. That's what I told myself. Over and over and over again. Sometimes it worked. Other times I ate chocolate.

When we find ourselves in coping mode, it is like running a marathon. There are the first few miles, where you feel like you can run all day. Then mile seven comes along and you feel like the run will never end. How will you ever survive? It is only in those last few miles that the realization you have accomplished this huge undertaking flashes into your awareness. It is in this moment that your biggest burst of energy finally emerges. The only way to truly tackle something so huge that coping becomes the norm is to concentrate on each step versus on the entire journey all at once.

Embracing uncertainty takes a lot of patience, and—like running a marathon—each step takes what it takes. You don't jump to mile 20 when you're at mile 7. You look down and notice methodically what each step feels like and then you stay there like a frozen TV dinner (similar to the crap my husband the heart patient ate in the hospital).

One of the people I interviewed along the way was a woman named Dr. Margaret Paul, who has a PhD and is the founder of an innovative therapeutic approach to mental well being called "Inner Bonding." In our interview we discussed the importance of taking responsibility for our inner lives.

"There are two kinds of feelings. There's the feelings we cause by what we call self abandonment. And that's judging ourselves staying in our head, going into addictions, making others responsible…that causes our anxiety, depression, guilt, shame, anger, aloneness, emptiness, and jealousy. And then there's another set of feelings that are the existential feelings of life. There's the wonderful feelings, the love, the joy, the peace. The painful feelings of loneliness, grief over loss or heartbreak when people are being mean to each other, or helplessness over other people and over events. Now, these are the feelings that we couldn't manage when we were little. They're big, big feelings. And I never saw any role modeling and people managing those feelings. And so I had to disconnect from those, like so many people and learn to do the addictive things that were actually creating my anxiety. But I didn't know that. This is why it's so important to learn to have a spiritual connection, because we can't manage those big feelings without love and without compassion. Love and compassion are not feelings we actually generate in our own bodies, we have to open to them, and invite them in," Dr. Paul shared.

I had to take responsibility for my inner psyche and tell myself that I was going to be okay. No one was able to invite that healing acknowledgement that *yes, this is tough but not impossible*, but me. And no one could concentrate on the *what-ifs* versus the *what is* but me.

PRAYER

On the morning of my husband's heart surgery—much like Queen Esther, who had asked the collective community to pray on her behalf—we asked our collective Beth Jacob Synagogue family to pray for Robbie. I knew it was the best chance we had to help turn Robbie's situation around. After I kissed him goodbye on his way to the OR, I took myself home to pray. "God, Let me know you have our backs. Don't let me down now, promise you'll give me the signs I need to know how to move through this crisis with grace, an open heart, and faith."

CHAPTER 15

NURTURING SURRENDER

At the start of my husband's illness, while I knew I could surrender to any outcome, I also wondered how I would surrender without feeling a sense of defeat. See, I hate surrender. Because, essentially, I hate defeat. And to me, surrendering felt like annihilation and defeat meant giving up. Just throwing your hands up in the air and saying, "There is nothing else I can do to change this outcome," felt like walking backwards on a tightrope. I don't really believe in defeat. And yet, while I don't believe you can interfere with the Divine charge, I do believe we are expected to become an agent to wield God's decisions into an outcome bathed in light and life's breath. And even though it may not turn into the outcome we want, we are still mandated by God's "life force rules" to fight tooth and nail to preserve life at all cost. Like the way I fought the hospital system and demanded Robbie get an IV while he burned with a one-hundred-and-five fever as his body was slowly withering away. So how does one walk the fine balance of surrendering our full selves while not giving into a defeatist mentality? Doesn't this seem completely contradictory?

Finding out my husband would be in the hospital for ten days for open-heart surgery—and without me getting to see him minutes before or after his heart was supposed to be cut open—felt impossible. The mitral valve replacement surgery is one of the most intensive surgeries. So much so, that the original cardiac surgeon our hospital booked Robbie with wound up canceling as soon as he heard it was a mitral valve replacement. He didn't feel qualified enough to undertake that surgery, which meant we had to wait yet another three weeks to get treated by the premier surgeon. And although we were grateful to have a wonderful surgeon, it also meant another three weeks to live with a weak heart that was just getting weaker by the day. It meant more time to wonder, would this be the last day? Would he wake up tomorrow morning?

The details around the mitral valve replacement surgery are maniacal. The patient is put to sleep, his chest sawed open, the heart is taken out of the body, sliced in half, then drained of any blood, and repaired all while the patient hovers in a quasi-living state on machines which simulate the heart muscle. Upon awakening, the patient is in the ICU for up to three days on life support. The heart takes time to regulate and the first twenty-four hours after a patient's open-heart surgery are the most critical.

Will the replacement work? Will the heart modulate? Will the patient survive?

Days before I was supposed to drop Robbie off at the hospital for his open-heart surgery, I received a few calls from several close friends and family members who could hear in my voice how frustrated I was about Robbie having to go through this big event without me being there by his side. With lots of good intention, I was told to "Be Positive… Have faith… Stop being so negative…." What most people did not really understand was that I was not negatively thinking about *outcome*. I knew Robbie and I would get through any outcome; we had the practice and the faith to forge through the unpredictabilities of life together. What had me up in arms was the thought that my husband was doing this big thing alone. After our last hospital stay coupled with generational trauma which made me fall into a deep place of quiet and sadness. I felt traumatized.

I was weary about handing the love of my life over to strangers. After our experience in the Las Vegas hospital—where he almost lost his life several times because healthcare workers did not know this patient or his baseline, and had neglected him, I was apprehensive that Robbie would be alone or in pain without an advocate. I didn't know a single person in the hospital who could be my stand-in while he underwent his stay during surgery. We did every single event in our adult lives together. Every one except the most important and vital event—a surgery that would determine the rest of his life. I remember my father after his open-heart surgery at the age of fifty-two. He was connected to tubes everywhere, on life support, in the ICU, awake, staring at my mother as she mouthed, "I love you." Several days later my parents announced their separation and I was left to take care of my dad while he recovered from a quadruple bypass.

I knew what the stakes were. But this was Robbie. My Robbie. This felt like an inconceivable battle. We were truly left to surrender to the only outcome we did not find optimal, which was to be apart during a grueling medical procedure and bank on God to protect Robbie during his two-week stay in the hospital. To make matters more difficult, there were several outcomes the doctor had made clear would be life-altering forever. We were walking into an unknown with no net to catch us other than God's will.

Here was what we were told: There are only two choices when undergoing a mitral valve replacement surgery. Neither of them are that great. There's a mechanical valve replacement, which, while it can last for many years, still comes with no guarantees. But it is a little better than the alternative bovine valve replacement, which only lasts ten years. The mechanical valve would make his heart click with a loud mechanical noise for the rest of his life. It would be like being married to the bionic man. I'd never hear his heartbeat the same way again. He would have to live with a constant clicking—like an amplified grandfather clock. It would also mean ongoing Coumadin treatment (a blood thinner) for the rest of his life. The therapeutics on that drug require weekly blood tests, severe threat of brain bleeding, and strokes. That would require being near a hospital forever, which would be a massive lifestyle change. There goes travel. While it's not an easy drug to be on, the other alternative meant Robbie might only get ten more years before needing another possible open-heart surgery, which at his fifty years of age was not optimal, ideal, or even feasible.

After a lot of decision making and option weighing, Robbie chose the Bovine valve to avoid the annoying loud clicking and the Coumadin. But it also meant, we were singing up for only ten years left together. ONLY ten more years. Ten years goes by quickly. But he was determined to have a good quality of life over a long arduous one. And maybe there would be an alternative, non-invasive surgery by then. Then again, maybe there wouldn't be.

Trauma told me I could not surrender. My fault lines started trembling. Back in 1959, when Grandpa Morton, my paternal grandfather, was only forty-two years old, he had a massive heart attack. My grandmother retold me this story numerous times throughout my life. How she went to visit him in the hospital, and her biggest regret was that she left that night, instead of crawling into bed and sleeping with him one last time. He could have died in her arms; instead he died alone. She got the call the very next morning that he'd been pronounced dead. For years I heard her retell this story with the sting of regret that ran through her tears.

I was not prepared to send my husband off for open-heart surgery. I was not prepared for us to face this big thing separated.handle my husband's surgery alone in quarantine without being right by his side. I was not prepared to have Robbie wake up alone. I was not prepared to not be the last person he went to sleep to before surgery and the first person he'd open his eyes to. If he died, he would die alone. I kept hearing friends and family say, "Chava, everything will be fine, you need to know that." But that was just not something that I knew. No one actually knew that. So I was forced to do the one and only thing I hated—I was forced to surrender.

I was sending my husband into heart surgery with an already barely beating one. The generational trauma of caring for the men in my family who had lost life and love because of their broken hearts coursed through me. I felt uneasy and slowly withered into my own cocoon of quiet.

The week before his surgery I turned off my phone. I went inward. I cried every day, for most of the day, until the day of surgery. I did not surrender quietly. I didn't cry because of the potentially frightening outcome we were facing, as much as I cried because we were facing this outcome without each other to hold onto. I could not imagine him waking up on a ventilator in the ICU, with no one familiar nearby. I could not imagine waking up to an empty bed for ten days and wondering if that bed would ever have his warm body back in it. I felt defeated. What was the point to this struggle? What was I not seeing? Soon my long crying fits turned into frenzies of questions as I began to work myself into a pretzel of wondering. What the hell was any of this suffering really for?

The first existential crisis the Bible reveals is in the book of Toldos when Rebekah learns she is carrying twin boys who will one day be dueling nations. The bible reads:

"But the children struggled in her womb, and she said, 'If so, why do I exist?' she went to inquire of the Lord."

The Stone edition bible translates the Hebrew text "If so, why do I exist?" to mean "If so, why am I thus?" In other words, "If so, what's my purpose?" She then continues her existential crisis later on after her son Esau announces his plans to murder his brother Jacob after he is duped out of his birthright. Rebekah's response is no less fatalistic, as she says to her husband, Isaac,

"I am disgusted with my life because of the Hittite women. If Jacob marries a Hittite woman like these, from among the native women, what good will life be to me?"

Knowing Rebekkah wants her values passed on to her offspring through Jacob and understanding this Hittite culture wouldn't be in alignment with her values, she gets pretty deep into lifeless despair. She's disgusted with her life? What good is her life? In other words, should her life not meet her expectations, and if she meets struggles she does not desire and that continue to cause her pain and suffering, what is the point of breathing at all?

The Hebrew word which translates to mean "disgusted" is "Katzti." The first letter of the word Katzti is actually quite smaller than the other letters in the text, which I found peculiar.

To further this odd episode, in the middle of Rebekah's crisis, she and her husband Isaac travel to the land of Gerar due to a famine in the land. Like Isaac's father Abraham, he winds up settling in King Abimelech's neighborhood. As the story goes, Isaac fails to tell Abimelech that Rebekah is his wife, for he fears the men of the palace might murder Isaac and ravage Rebekah. If he acts as her brother, he feels he has better leverage to protect them both. Later the king learns Isaac and Rebekah are indeed married when it says in the passage,

"...Abimelech King of the Philistines gazed down through the window and saw—Behold! Isaac was jesting with his wife Rebecca."

Upon Abimelech seeing Rebekah as Isaac's wife, he not only embraces the couple but offers them protection and even goes so far as to announce them as part of his royal court. I find it unusual that we need the seemingly minute detail that Abimelech gazed out of his window and then finally saw Rebekah as Isaac's wife. What was the point of telling us he looked out a window?

Rebekah was struggling to understand the purpose of life amongst the struggle. She was distraught over and over by her circumstances. This inner fight of Esau and Jacob is compared in the Kabbalah to the fight one has between their physical and their spiritual selves. Essentially Rebekah was asking, how do I find power in my spirit when my corporeal needs are ignored? If my sons fight, if one son is murdered by the other, if I cannot control who my son Jacob marries, if my grandchildren do not hold my values near to their heart—then what is the point of living? What is the point to living a meaningful existence when I can't control all the variables and possible meaningless outcomes?

And then suddenly King Abimelech looks out the window and he gets a glimpse of her—the true her—standing there in all her power and her truth. And he is in awe—so much so that he announces her royalty along with Isaac's royalty and warns his people not to *"molest this man or his wife or they will surely be put to death."* For when you are in struggle and yet you still seize your life with gusto and love—it is then your body and soul are finally, completely united and you can awaken your truth. Maybe the window was a metaphor to the king seeing something no one else could see, not even Rebekah herself. It took someone else to see her, really see her story and peer through the "looking glass" to finally get a glimpse of her ultimate, transcendent power.

When Rebekah's son Jacob held on to Esau's heel upon their birth, the Bible was telling us that you can never truly get away from the inner torment of life's struggle. There will always be a small part, even the size of a heel, that stays grounded inside the world of resistance and struggle. And you can search and yearn for ease, but ease will never remain. To be alive is to be in a state of grappling discovery. Discovery of what it all means, of why we are here, of what we can do to repair the world. This is the job. This is what we are called on to live for. It's called the pursuit of existence, and it is noble and ever evolving. Although we scramble and yearn for the world of ease, for every part of us wants ease, our heel will still remain forced by the cosmos to innovate, escalate our transformation and walk us through life's struggle with an eager determination. And that pursuit is in itself a meaningful one—despite any outcome it may come with.

Perhaps the word *Katzti*, where Rebekah says how "disgusted" she is with her life's journey, stems from the root word *Katz* which translates to mean "end." Meaning, she reached the end. Sometimes the struggle is too much to bear. You reach the end. And the first letter in this word is small because that's how one must feel when it's too much—small and humble when all there is left is to surrender to the greater force—God himself. And in that moment we are small, yet not insignificant. There's a humility that must happen to move through that struggle.

It was becoming clearer to me that to battle through the agony of earth-shattering trauma, I had to become quiet. I let myself slip into the silence to finally hear the sound of clarity I yearned to find. I was not defeated, for I was not giving up. Surrendering became my victory dance. It was my way of tinkering inside the control room with purpose and conviction to make room for the ascendance to a Higher Power. Like Rebekkah, I had finally reached my end, but I could not be disgusted by the outcome no matter what transpired. I had to peer through the window of my own eyes and know deeply that I, too, could stand in my power and I would not be alone.

Still, I hate surrender.

CHAPTER 16

NURTURING THAT WRENCH
IN THE WORKS

A wrench in the works happens when somewhere, seemingly out of nowhere, the Universe heaves a hunk of disruption right at your cerebral cortex. You didn't ask for it—in fact, you never even saw it coming. In some ways, trauma is the ultimate wrench in the works.

It is literally impossible to write a book on nurturing ourselves back to being okay, without talking about the elephants in the room: stress, anxiety, shock, strain, TRAUMA. As I wrote this chapter back in 2020, musing on the inner workings of how trauma, grief, and faith dance together to the tune of surrender, I was sitting at the bedside of my 100-year-old Grandpa, (Papa) Richie, who was dying from old age. Sitting with my Pop was not really a wrench in the works as much as an expected outcome to life.

I truly believe we're going to need faith if we are going to fully nurture our grief and trauma to a place of restoration. This is a process I have worked on for many years, but have not always gotten right. There have been many many times my grief became my focus and compass instead of my faith. To truly understand how a case of misguided faith shaped the way I fabulously misunderstood grief, we must begin with the year 1978.

In 1978, on the high holiday of Rosh Hashanah, my parents drove my brother and I up to be with our grandparents. That holiday was going to be special because "The Blue Bubby," Grandpa Richie's mother, was going to be joining us. We called her The Blue Bubby because she dyed her hair a grayish-blue hue that reminded us all of her age and her vanity.

I was only two-and-a-half years old, but I remember this experience precisely. This was my first wrench in the works. You don't forget your first wrench.

When we arrived at Grandma Bettie and Papa Richie's house, I went straight to the living room. My baby brother, Yaakov, was only too happy to crawl around on the floor and stretch his legs after the two-hour drive, the Blue Bubby napped quietly on the sofa, and I went to my favorite piece of furniture. It was an antique side table that had three levels with tiny, mesh-wired doors holding a few knickknacks. I used to imagine that the first level of this table was my stage; the second level was the podium, which held my speech, and the tiny doors held my congregation's Torah.

I was the rabbi in charge of this place, and sang with great fervor as my congregants (Yaakov and the napping Blue Bubby) paid attention to my sermon and holy words. Behind that brilliant piece of furniture was the stone fireplace with a hearth that looked like a stage. I know what you're thinking, and many of my congregants also wondered: why didn't I use the hearth to conduct my sermons? The answer is because this hearth was frightening. It was made up of hard sedimentary slate that was stone cold and very uncomfortable to stand on with my bare feet. The grooves of the stone pinched my little toes and scratched my delicate skin. I hated this fireplace and always figured it was a terrible hazard.

I can still see the fibers on the carpet dancing to the wind of the heater. It was around then I learned that old people like their homes warmer than a wooden sauna, which reminds their sweat glands that they haven't expired yet.

Grandma Bettie had taken many precautions to keep her house safe. For example, she installed marble coffee tables in the family room, which came up to my *temple* and reached Yaak's two-week-old set of *teeth*. But don't worry—she piled loads of magazines on top, hoping the high-gloss pages would be a good enough cushion in case I ever split my cerebrum on the sharp corner. The knick knacks on her *glass* coffee table in the living room consisted of a metal bird with a sharp tail, a tall bronze candlestick that was heavier than a steel machete, and a pair of green grapes carved out of marble. Surprisingly, she also had wax fruit lying in a golden basket. To say I didn't try to eat those perfectly rotund wax grapes would be lying.

The fact was, I had chosen the safest thing in the house to play on. That soft wooden antique side table became my playhouse, Synagogue, and Holy Ark all rolled into one. While I was in the middle of my discourse of what color God was, the Blue Bubby woke up.

The whole thing happened in an instant. I don't know why I knew what was about to happen before it happened. And I don't know why none of the other adults took notice of the fact that a two-and-half year-old playing alone near her baby brother with zero adult supervision, other than a ninety-year-old woman, in a dangerous living room was not a potential hazardous situation waiting to implode. (When I find out that answer, we can write another whole book on the matter of adulting responsibly.) The Blue Bubby got up and, in an effort to avoid stepping on me, she tripped and slammed her fragile, aged skull onto that stone fireplace and cracked her head open. The next thing I remember was a series of sounds and images: screaming (probably my own), yelling (my mother), crying (my baby brother), blood dripping down the corner of the hearth, lights flashing, my Papa Richie putting down his glass of vodka, my Grandma Bettie bending over to grab the Blue Bubby, hands wringing, pacing, and then various handsome firemen and paramedics storming into *the castle of doom.*

The Blue Bubby was wheeled out of the house on a gurney. She was hardly conscious, and I was sure that I had killed her. I was also sure my stint as a rabbi was forever over, and I would never have the opportunity to give my last goodbye speech to my congregants or inspire others using my faith again. Who wants to have a grandma killer for a clergyman?

Two weeks later, after undergoing brain surgery, the Blue Bubby died. My father said she died of old age. But guilt had racked up pretty good inside my little head. I had already begun to build the narrative around faith and grief at that tender toddler age. I had to do anything I could to stop the Universe from seeking its revenge on me after I killed the Blue Bubby. I became obsessed with avoiding God's wrath. I didn't see my Higher Power as loving; I saw Him as a vengeful, scary alien in the sky waiting to strike me for my sin. I was little Chava who had left Eden that day and wondered if I would ever be allowed back.

My parents were from a very secular Jewish background. They did not have the answers to explain how faith or God worked. So I never told them what my own crazy narrative had become. After sending me to a Jewish day school at the age of six, we began to take on more observances. My dad worked on the weekends, so in an effort to keep us kids busy, my mom took us to spend Shabbat afternoons with our observant friends. Those afternoon visits eventually turned into my parents eating Friday night dinner together, attending Synagogue regularly, and observing our faith in a weekly fashion (versus the bi-annually we had come to know).

By the time I was ten, I believed that I had become religious; just like Eve, my namesake. And just like Eve had been banished from the garden for her sin, I believed I had been banished from the garden for my sin of killing the Blue Bubby.

I was a crafty little thing who was able to convince my parents that religion would be our saving grace from ever experiencing pain again. I was able to manipulate situations. "Mom, could we go to Synagogue?" [Distraction.] "Let's host a Torah in our home for two years!" [Distraction.] "Can we have only glatt milk and meat?" [Distraction.] I even insisted that my family stay home for twenty-five consecutive hours with pre-cut toilet paper each week—a failing, miserable distraction. (Jews don't tear on the Sabbath…hence the pre-cut T.P) The reason why I say this was all a distraction is because in my heart, I believed faith *was a protective distraction:* something I could wave in front of God to keep Him from punishing me for my Blue Bubby sin.

It would take me many more years to understand that faith is not a deal. It is not a bargain to trade for a life free from struggle. Faith does not stop you from experiencing traumatic events; it is merely the vehicle to help you survive and eventually prevail when trauma hits. If you're alive you're sure to experience big hard stuff. That is inevitable. No one is getting out of this thing called life alive. No one. And yet, I believed I could beat God at His own game. I believed I didn't need faith to heal me from my fears of living through the big scary stuff. Instead, I used my wounded self as an excuse to not have to evolve.

When I was little, my faith was founded on the preposterous idea that if I took on more commandments, God might not "get me." For me, calling myself "religious" felt like getting caught saying a dirty word. The shame I had associated with the expression of how I kept my faith (rather faith-LESS, cowering in fear) began to erode my soul. It's as if the word "religious" became THE dirty word. For I did not associate the word 'religious' with piety; rather, I had begun to associate the word "religious" with cynicism and falseness. As I got older, I began to understand how broken my narrative had become. I falsely believed I should have been impervious to the struggles of faith because of my role as faith's protector. After all, I was a rabbi's wife! Shouldn't I have known better? And Yet. I was lost. I didn't understand how faith and grief could interact and coincide.

In my Jewish faith, I was taught to believe that every single event is Divinely orchestrated. And yet when that orchestration took a dark turn, I automatically imagined that turn was the result of me not measuring up to my Creator. That sometimes left me wondering if I even had a Creator at all. I was a rabbi's wife, I had taken an oath to lead in faith, yet I felt uncomfortable calling myself faithful. I felt like a fraud, but I was determined to discover my truth even if only for the sake of being of service to others. And then the second wrench in the works came barreling down at me, and the lesson began to take shape.

I was thirty-five when I began to experience death at an irregular pace. Up until that point, I had actually never seen a dead person *(technically, I did not see the Blue Bubby dead; I only saw her wounded),* unless you count my dog Trapper who had an epileptic seizure and drowned in our pool when I was five years old.

(Losing a pet is a seriously sad thing to go through, which is why, years later, my friend Stefanie received 37 facebook condolences when her dog died. My friend David, whose mother passed away that same week, only got 5.)

There's a reason I became a writer/filmmaker/singer and not a paramedic, doctor, or funeral director. I don't do blood and guts. I NEVER watch horror films. However, at the age of thirty-five, privileged to have spent so many years free from the disruption of death (again, I was *religious*), I sat with three people as they died and attended TEN funerals within an eighteen-month period.

I sat with my Uncle Doug as he died from brain cancer on my birthday. He was fifty-eight. I sang hymns to my Grandma Bettie as she died on my birthday, one year later. Six of the people we mourned were dear friends. There was my sister-in-law's niece, Shula, who died at the tender age of three in an automobile accident the same week we sat with her licking ice cream on a street corner in New York. There was my daughter's best friend, fifteen-year-old Tsofia; our fearless friend, Chris, who was only fifty; our good friend's twenty-two-year-old son, who drowned a week after he got engaged. There was Uncle Alan, who was fifty-eight when he collapsed and died out of nowhere on a bike ride. There was Robbie's father, who died from cancer at sixty-four.

And finally there was my father who died at sixty. Umm, are you getting the picture here yet?

Aside from my Grandma Bettie, all of these deaths were either children, twenty-something-year-olds, or adults under the age of sixty. Only two of the deaths were people who were ill; the rest were so sudden they left the living in shock and awe. I was living this *religious life*. I had made so many changes in how I observed my faith since that Blue Bubby incident. Yet my perfect dream still fell apart. I had turned my back on the greatest, most fundamental essence of what an enlightened person lives to become. I drank the Kool-Aid. I had not internalized the punch. I lived in anger and fear and with the perpetual narrative that these deaths could have been stopped—that with enough prayer something, anything could have been done to stop them from happening. My arrogance had me believing that because I had taken an oath to lead with faith, because I had "done everything right," I and those around me were impervious to ever experiencing pain. Which made me resent my grief and my faith even more.

And then the day arrived. It was a sunny afternoon, and I was filling my days with as many distracting creative projects as I could muster in the aftermath of my grief storm, when my mother called to check on me.

Mom: *Chava, are you getting out of bed yet?*

(I'd become an expert at writing and creating in bed.)

Me: *What's the point? God is going to be angry at me forever for what happened when I was two.*

Mom: "*What do you mean…what happened when you were two?*"

Me: "*Mom, we don't have to re-hash this. I'm a grown-up now. We both know what happened.*"

Mom: "*Chava, what are you referring to?*"

Me [in a whisper]: "*You know, when I was banished from Eden because I—I killed the Blue Bubby.*"

Mom: "*Chava, how could you think that all these bad things have happened because of what happened to Bubby?*"

Me: "*Because…I know God! He and I have a thing. He's clearly punishing me and every person I come in contact with. I must be cursed or something.*"

My mom began to laugh so hard. Guilt has a funny way of allowing your brain to be hijacked by idiotic stories. Finally, my mom stopped laughing long enough to say,

Mom: "*Chava, are you kidding me? Bubby didn't fall because she tripped over you!*"

Me: "*What?*"

Mom: "*No! It was your brother. You didn't kill the Blue Bubby, he probably did.*"

And that's how I finally woke up. A little laughter and a dose of my mom's irreverent sense of humor and suddenly a narrative I'd carried around since toddlerhood was finally deconstructed.

The Halley's Comet of knowing had arrived. And then The Rock came to me in a dream and said, *"Chava, this is your wake up call, get your ass UP. (Also call your brother. He should know what he did.)"* Then he handed me a fire rifle and I jumped off a building with a parachute attached. I had nothing left to do but either get up and claw my way through the trauma or literally lay down underneath it forever. So the work began. Yes, Halley's Comet forced its way down my street, aimed itself at my house, and yelled, *"Here's your wrench in the works! Take notice!"* But it also did something else. It left enough space in its wake to allow me to rewrite the script.

It was time to stop blaming myself for a childhood event that I was not responsible for. It was time to stop seeing God as the mean alien ready to strike. Instead of being led by faith, I was being led by fear. Instead of seeing faith as my saving grace, I blamed it for allowing death into my orbit without the invitation I arrogantly felt it required.

So no, I am not—nor have I ever been—a Blue Bubby Killer. Nor am I really responsible for all bad things that have happened to all good people. This is real life. And in this real life we can blame everything on my brother, Yaak. *Just kidding!* It's not his fault either. That fall had been written in the Blue Bubby's script from her birth. We all have a script. And we all have a role to play in it. After that conversation with my mom, it was evident how ridiculous my old narrative around faith and God had become. When we are children we have a visual of what God looks like. Sometimes, if we are not careful, we can keep that visual going into adulthood.

I believe painful events have the capacity to teach us how to lean into life with more depth and awareness. Much of grief comes from the picture we have created of our lives not matching the reality we are in. We constantly compare the picture to reality, and if we don't accept the new moment as it is, our grief worsens. There are times our journey has to stop to tend to it.

Carrying grief around is like carrying a backpack of rocks up Mount Kilimanjaro; some days it can feel heavy and other times it is barely detectable. There are moments it can feel like the albatross bearing down on our small frames as we tire past the deep bluff, and other times the road flattens and we can barely feel its weight bearing down on our shoulders. And those are the times we readjust our spectacles to the new movie we are in. That's when the grief gets lessened just a little bit. These difficult experiences are also my gift, which has made me stronger while I wander through the open seas of anguish.

When that wrench in the works arrived, it knocked another knowing into me. The new knowing was having awareness of my own strength, despite the grief that now inhabited my body.

While I didn't like it, a veil was lifted, and suddenly I found myself peeking into the inner workings of the world differently—with more wisdom, with more insight. Before that knowing happened, my idealism was intact. My naiveté coddled me like spider silk; malleable yet unbreakable. The void that occurs when grief sets in has us feeling like our heart will be broken forever. But it also reveals truths. They might be truths we were hoping we'd never have to learn…but I'm so happy I did learn them.

What is a broken heart? It is a deep void in your body that remains where an unconditional, accepting love once lived. What do we fill this void with? Sometimes we fill the void with destructive habits, depression, or bitterness. Instead of inhabiting the space with beauty and acceptance, we can fill it with desolation and bleakness. That's what grief does when it is not harnessed: it creeps into the crevices of your new empty space and it disrupts the entire ecosystem. It can swallow your heart whole if you let it. However, that hole left by the love of someone who has died can never be banished. It is there forever. And at some point, as my Bubby Shirley used to say, "You gotta make a choice. You can either fill that space with more love or fill it with anger and bitterness."

Once, while I was struggling to handle my grief and loss, a man who lost his seventeen-year-old daughter to cancer said to me, "You must not think of the people who have died as those we have lost. If you had a relationship with that person, nothing is ever lost. They are just in a different room. You can still experience their love. It's just different now."

In other words, he was giving me permission to keep on loving. Which is why after mourning my father for a good year, I finally turned to my kids (then fourteen, eleven, and eight) and I said. "I want to thank you for putting up with my sadness. I am done now. I am going to fill this space up with loving you guys with all of my being."

I sat at my Grandpa Richie's deathbed. I was lucky; this was a privilege many people had not had during the past years. The nurse came in and said his oxygen was dropping. The blotchy red discoloration on his legs indicated he was not getting blood to his extremities. His hands were swollen. He refused food and water. I felt him leaving and hanging on with the weight of his labored breathing. While he was not conscious, he still moaned in the direction of my voice. Our love orbited his small room filled with the stench of death. And I was positive it would continue to do so even after his last breath.

I have come to see the hole from grief as a gift. The bigger the hole we experience, the bigger the love once weighed. As my good friend Dina Hurwitz once said to me while caring for her husband, who suffers with ALS, "The greater we love, the more excruciating the pain of loss becomes. If you're lucky, it's really excruciating."

That void is also the prompt that allows us to learn about love. It compels us to wonder what space we fill in other people's hearts. We search for our own meaning; we wonder how we are contributing to this loving cosmic engine. And it is through that search that the grief becomes less heavy and the void becomes less empty.

Grief is the reminder to take notice of and re-evaluate our own truths and values. It can remind us we have the ability to crawl back into that utopia called Eden to reinvent our existence with the full love that once inhabited our bodies—and that we can allow that love to spread and grow. The room in your heart can become the place where more love and understanding extends to others.

Our post-pandemic world got to know the empty space very well. The one complaint we all had was the deafening silence. A hush rolled into our cities during lockdown. When a person dies, the silence of not hearing that person's voice is deafening. And yet, if you are very, very quiet and slip underneath it, listening to the beating of your own heart, I believe their heart song can be heard again.

Many of us have stared down trauma, even tried laughing at it— yet there it stands, taunting us into believing it cannot be repaired. Sometimes we might wonder if the void from our losses will ever be filled or if it will remain deeply embedded in us like a cut that won't heal.

It will heal, if we allow it to, but we should also be aware that while grief might leave, it also quietly floats. Some days we hear it whooshing and rumbling through us, other days it is quiet. But it is always there, pulsing. There are two stages to grief: the heavy grief and the lighter grief. The goal is to get to the place where the lighter grief lives.

So how do you move through to the lighter grief? Here is a list of things not to try:

1. Ignore your grief or trauma.
2. Deny it by never talking about it or acknowledging it.
3. Distract yourself from it using any available means.

These might sound appealing, but in my considerable experience, all three of these approaches will only prolong the period of heavy grief and the pain that trauma might inhabit.

Unfortunately, the only way to heal your trauma and grief is to move through it. Here is another list. The to-do list. These things are harder and less appealing, but they will allow your grief to dissipate (or at least become tolerable):

1. Speak about your traumatic events and your grief.
2. Connect to others who are suffering through a similar experience.
3. Hold space for others who also need to have their pain seen. Reach out to those grieving, especially if you have a story to share about the person they lost. Just don't share about your own personal loss. The grieving person needs to know their struggle is real without the burden of holding your grief as well. Share how that person who they are mourning impacted your life. That is the greatest gift

one can give to someone grieving. To know their person left an impact. To know their story is still living on in others' lives.

Many of us are suffering. Folks have died and lost loved ones because of war, the pandemic, or other natural disasters. Some have lost their jobs. Many of us have suffered severe pain because of weathering illness, dealing with the constant churn of uncertainty, and tackling the pain of racial discrimination. The global list of reasons to grieve seem to be endless.

During the period of my life that was filled with so many losses, I wondered if I would ever emerge from that dark place. I wanted there to be some meaning I could glean from the constant barrage of loss that just kept crashing down over and over. The one thing I held onto was a tiny, albeit sometimes cynical, kernel of faith. I truly believed that God could still create miracles, and that one day He would reach out and carry me with a message of hopeful optimism.

The year the pandemic rolled in, my brother Yaakov and I, without knowing it, each decided to read the entire book of Psalms twice on the first night of the Jewish New Year. Which meant that on that Rosh Hashanah holiday we read it four times altogether.

Back when I was struggling to make sense of all our losses I asked a lot of "why's" and "how can you's" to God. I got a lot of silence. But then in the middle of the greatest global crisis of the 21st century, on my daughter's Hebrew birthday, my 18th nephew was born. In Hebrew the number eighteen is read as the word "Chai," which translates to mean "life." I don't think it's coincidental that on the day before 9-11-2020, God blessed my family with CHAI, with LIFE. I deeply understand that those dark days were heavy, but I also feel like the message God sent our family which we so desperately needed was that they are also finite. Suffering cannot and does not last forever. What can be infinite is believing in an unlimited Higher Power that knows how to mend the darkness.

Death is a devastating pain—one that cannot be explained, interpreted, or rationalized, and I'm not trying to rationalize it. But I see something for the first time so clearly. I believe we are all part of this narrative of death and it is literally gripping us in a chokehold. I think there's more than meets the eye when it comes to our existence and to what happens when our bodies expire.

The Zohar (Kabbalah) describes the physical world as built on four separate worlds. Each one is a bubble of light that slowly emerges from the next one to the next one until God's light has finally dimmed into the world we are in. Our world is the one with physical form, standing on its own with only God's dim and hidden light. The Zohar explains that God created this physical world with these four worlds behind it in order to slowly remove His powerful light from every world so that physicality can be inhabited on its own. God's light is so strong, that in order for the physical world to exist He needed to contract Himself otherwise the entire world would be filled with Godly light, and the material world would be obsolete. The four worlds are the process of that contraction. Each world inhabits a little bit less Godly light and that unlimited energy, to finally get to the world we inhabit, where God exists, but can't be seen. Where the energy is still in control of the world, yet contracted just enough to allow our own will to exist. Making us separate yet deeply connected. That is why it feels like His elusive energy can be grasped and yet not attained at the same time. He is us, and we are Him, but in His most compassionate display of love. He has also made room for us to be ourselves as distinct entities with our own free will.

The purpose of God removing His light to attain this extreme physical state where we can't see him at all is because He wants us to create our own light. If the light is already created, then there is nothing for us to achieve. However, if we are charged to dig deep even in pain and darkness, then our faith not only matters—it is ever more powerful and required. When we manage to create our own unique light, that is when the repair begins. God wishes to see His own world the way a father or mother births a child with the hopes of seeing their values and ideals unfold in a separate entity. Separate, yet embodying His essence; apart, yet joined in our efforts.

When we're hit with a wrench in the works, it's usually to point out something we needed real clarity on, or a calling to step up toward growth. For me, I needed to massively redefine how I see faith as my tool. I needed to redefine Eden. Finding God was never supposed to interrupt my life or keep me from experiencing pain; it was supposed to support and assist me, giving me skills to face my fears.

I have met a new God, a compassionate one. My God is like George Burns. He tells jokes. He is not a mean alien living in the sky, with squinty eyes and a lighting rod, waiting to pounce on me.

In the beginning of his work *The Guide for the Perplexed*, Rabbi Moshe Ben Maimon, Maimonidies (1135-1204), one of the greatest philosophers and personalities in Jewish history, raises a question in response to the most misinterpreted story in the book of Genesis. Adam and Eve's little snack from the Tree of Knowledge between Good and Bad created an upheaval that not only banished them from the Garden of Eden, but created a world where death and pain became part of human existence. At the same time, the knowledge that Adam and Eve acquired, although burdensome, also enlightened them and took them out of their naïve innocence forever. As the serpent argued before he seduced Eve into eating the fruit, "God knows that on the day you eat from it, your eyes will be opened, and you will be like God, knowing good and bad" Ibid. 3:5. Following the eating from the tree, the story continues, "God said, 'Man has now become like the Unique One among us, knowing good and bad'" Ibid. 3:22.

Maimonides claims that this event was not a curse, but rather the greatest blessing that humanity could have been given. Suddenly human beings were no longer animals reacting on instinct, but autonomous creatures who could understand the difference between good and evil and choose. They were mature beings with Divine knowledge and wisdom designed to reshape their existence.

The enigmatic serpent is not a destructive force here, creating desolation and sorrow; it is God's mysterious hand pushing us into the sea of life to help us learn the lesson that we are born with the strength inside of us to prevail despite life's difficulties. The apple was meant to show us how to live with the dichotomy of good and bad, hope and despair, happiness and sadness—faith and fear.

Maybe Eve was meant to make her mistake. Maybe we can finally stop blaming her for humanity's entire downfall. *Maybe I can stop blaming myself.* Can it be that Eve's apple represents human fallacy, that her paradise represents human hope, and that her downfall represents human growth? Maybe we are all meant to fall from Eden and recreate our own paradise in the new world we learn to inhabit.

Although I was born during a blizzard, and sat with two people as they took their last breath on my birthday (Did I mention that happened twice? TWICE.), I can still look faith in the eye. I can still find a way to experience these events as purely privileged connections to the Divine. I have been privileged to witness birth and death, which is no small feat. To experience consciousness leaving, and consciousness staying, is truly a gift. When my Pop finally took his last breath, I was reading the entire book of David's

Psalms and when I got to the last word, he stopped breathing. He was 100.

The gift of faith is that even while you are grieving, while the heaviness surrounds you, you are imbued with the power to transform. With faith, you can transform in spite of the pain—maybe because of the pain. So I can finally admit without apology that I am not religious at all. Rather, I am working on becoming a transformer.

A transformer is a person who allows grief and disappointment to evolve and revolutionize their faith, to deconstruct their misplaced narratives, to ultimately transcend past victimhood. A transformer is ever-evolving, always maturing, forever adapting. Just call me a card-carrying transformer who can stand in a blizzard with her wet galoshes, unafraid and undaunted. (Ahh, now being born in a blizzard all makes sense.) As my father always said growing up, "A religious person is afraid of going to hell. A transformer has been to hell and back already."

I think we are all on a path toward something enlightening, toward something transforming, whether we are ready for it or not. The *wrench in the works* calls upon us so we have the opportunity to see something we didn't see before. It reclaims our attention and begs us to reveal it in ourselves and in this world. Don't be scared of the wrench—it's cool stuff.

Like a caterpillar who struggles out of her small cocoon, only to emerge in her new shape as a beautiful butterfly, we had our own metamorphosis because of our critical life events, and indeed, we became beautiful.

It is time to really live life. To redefine Eden, to brush ourselves off, and climb back into God's garden—one step at a time.

CHAPTER 17

ONE SMALL STEP

When I was a child, my father started a ritual that will stay with me forever. In the early days of his physician's residency, he would get home from moonlighting at the hospital in the middle of the night. (My brother remembers thinking that "moonlighting" meant my dad was an astronaut who healed sick people in space.) Ta would wake my little brother and me up before the sun came up and whisper into our ears, "Come on, we're gonna go see dawning."

He would then drive us in his Datsun at four o'clock in the morning right down to the pier. He'd buy us spicy chili for breakfast to keep the morning chill from freezing our small bones. And together, we would watch the purple crest rise in the east. The sun would come up over the coastline, and that was dawning. When my other siblings were born, he would venture out with them too. While on our summer breaks, my father was the first one up during our family beach vacations to escort us little ones to dawning.

This is by far my sweetest childhood memory. But it is only recently that I have discovered a deeper wisdom to Ta's dawning.

Because my father lost his dad when he was nine years old, he used to lament that the hardest thing about being an orphan at such a young age was the constant feeling that he was not like the other children. He always said he hated being different, and he wished he could remember his father better. Mostly, he hated the looks of pity.

When he was in his thirties and began searching for purpose and spiritual meaning, he was very much attracted to Chabad Chassidic philosophy as a result of the relationship he was privileged to have with Rabbi Menachem Mendel Schneerson, the Lubavitcher Rebbe. The Chabad Chassidic philosophy is grounded in the idea that strengthening our intellect has the power to drive our emotional state and awaken our transcendental mind. My father was drawn to the Rebbe because he was deeply impressed with the Rebbe's resolve and ability to overcome adversity and transform it into purpose and action. Without oversimplifying the Rebbe's approach to difficult situations, it was about mind over matter and using positive energy and action to manifest better outcomes.

My father told me on more than one occasion that the Rebbe's ability to connect with him filled the void he'd had for so many years as a result of not having a father.

Rabbi Gershon Jacobson (May 30, 1934 - May 29, 2005) was the founder and editor of a Yiddish newspaper known as *The Algemeiner Journal,* founded in New York, which is distributed to this day in English. Rabbi Jacobson made it his mission to keep the Jewish community informed of worldly events pertaining to the Jewish people. Shortly after the Second World War, before the fall of the Iron Curtain, the Lubavitcher Rebbe sent Rabbi Jacobson to Russia for the sake of reporting on the condition of the Jewish community, which at that time was grim.

Rabbi Jacobson spent weeks collecting stories and writing down each person's Jewish name on his own body, since recording them on paper would have been considered an act of espionage. Upon arriving back in New York, he read each Jewish name along with their mother's name from his limbs, and asked the Rebbe to pray on their behalf. Rabbi Jacobson spent all night sharing stories of Russian Jewry and their struggles with keeping their faith privately so as not to offend the communist regime. However, one story in particular brought tears to the Rebbe's eyes, and caused him much anguish and sadness—feelings the Rebbe rarely allowed himself to indulge in.

A small child had gone to public school one day, and instead of being given the typical ration of potatoes for lunch, that day his class was offered ice cream. The child's mother had warned him not to partake in the ice cream because it wasn't kosher. The child wept and asked, "But mama, I get nothing to eat all day, why can't I eat the ice cream like the other children?"

It was this story out of all the rest that had the Rebbe sobbing. His sensitivity to a child's innocent request was the story that crushed the Rebbe's spirit. However, as the Rebbe looked outside and saw the sun coming up, he slammed his hand on the desk, dried his eyes, and pronounced, "It is morning. No more tears."

Kabbalists have said that sunrise is the ultimate transition. It is this transition that teaches us the ability to leap into a new day, a new existence. We have the power to transform our pain from victimized moons, reflecting the wounds of time in our darkest hour, into suns who can shine on our own.

Dawning is that bittersweet, Godly whisper telling us something very precious must leave us in order to make room for something new. Dawning is the perfect expression of recovery and revival. It is God's answer to growth, His ultimate comfort.

The morning I rose from Shiva after the loss of my father, I woke up to the sun hitting my face, and a terrible fear swelled inside me. How would I go on? How would I transition to a new day without my father physically with me? How would I live normally? I closed my eyes and remembered driving through the night with my family just eleven days earlier. It was the 13th of Av, Shabbat Nachamu, known as the Sabbath of Comfort. I recalled the silence of the night and the monotonous ten-hour drive. But at four a.m., I looked out the car window and watched the birth of the early morning and I called my brother who was driving in the car ahead of me and said, "Yaakov, look outside, it is dawning."

"I know," he said. "I see it too. I see it too."

Every day we can make the decision to see our lives through the powerful lens of dawning. We don't have to make massive changes; they can be small.

In the Book of Genesis, in the portion entitled Vayeshev, Joseph was thrown into a pit by his brothers. Later, he was found, sold into slavery, and then falsely accused of raping his master's wife. Thrown into prison for a crime he didn't commit, uncertain of how long he might serve his prison sentence or its ultimate outcome, Joseph teaches us the greatest lesson in how we are to conduct ourselves during uncertain times, even AFTER the chips have fallen.

Every person in Joseph's life other than his father had abandoned him, and his father thought he was dead. He saw no way out of his terrible fate. His uncertainty was at the highest level. However, the text hints at the uplifting state of mind Joseph insisted on inhabiting despite his difficult and uncertain fate.

There were two men in jail alongside him, a butler and a baker. They both had terrible dreams, leaving them dismayed. What happens next is nothing short of inspiring.

The verse says Joseph approached the men and asked them, "Why do you look so sadly today?" Such an odd question. They're all in a dungeon. They're living their worst life. Bad dream or not, they're going to wake up looking like hell…they're uncertain, stressed out, and full of anxiety. Yet Joseph is bewildered. Because no matter what was going on and how uncertain things were in Joseph's life, he still chose to reflect joy. He had purpose and that gave him joy. I think the Torah was so specific about Joseph's words, "Why do you look so sadly today?" on purpose. These words are there to teach us how to handle difficult and uncertain experiences. German writer and philosopher, Eckert Tolle writes that "Surrender means acceptance. Acceptance initiates healing. The foundation for healing is to accept this moment as it is."

And that's essentially what Joseph did. He accepted his fate with gratitude and joy, he leaned into the discomfort. If you want to know your future, look into your past, and then re-adjust your present. Often, when we want to look into our future, we imagine it is quite daunting. We can look into our past, and remember the hard times we never thought we'd survive, but did with grace. Then we can look at our present and think, "I can do this. I've done it before, I can do it again. I am doing it right now." That's resilience. Resilience is the ability to put one foot in front of the other with methodical courage.

In May of 1942, a handful of American soldiers were chosen for an elite Battalion known as Merrill's Marauders. They were assigned to one of the most dangerous missions behind Japanese lines in Burma. The men fought leeches, snakes, constant hunger, fever, malaria, bloody dysentery, scrub typhus, and, of course, their enemy—the Japanese soldiers. They climbed through the steep Burmese mountains, toiling through mud, fog, heat, humidity, and rain in order to reach the Japanese airfield and destroy it, ending Japan's combative edge. It was the most daring mission the United States deployed. After five months of combat, 95 percent of the battalion were either dead, wounded, or unfit for combat.

My late grandfather was part of the elite medical Battalion which accompanied Merrill's Marauders as they forged through the war-torn, treacherous mountains of Burma to bring medical treatment to the Chinese and American soldiers. My grandfather suffered from starvation and malaria. Ten years after the war, at the age of 42, he died of a heart attack—possibly as a result of weathering those harsh conditions in the Burmese mountains—leaving my grandmother a widow at the tender age of thirty-six with three small children. My father was only nine years old. Grandpa Morton Shallman was a United States Lieutenant Corporal, and was chosen for this battalion because of his unique training to maneuver through mountainous terrain. According to my grandfather's brother, Uncle Billy, "Your grandfather pulled more teeth than any man alive because of all the Chinese soldiers and Burmese civilians with bad oral hygiene."

My grandfather was an oral surgeon, but performed many other life-saving procedures on the battlefield. There were many accounts of medics performing surgery with bullets whizzing overhead; the constant barrage from the Japanese front was as incessant as it was relentless during his time in the battalion. There he was assigned to heal others as his own life hung in the balance.

According to Charlton Ogburn Jr., who was the only Merrill's Marauder to write a memoir, *The Marauders*, "The worst thing, was the suspense. You never knew from one moment to the next when you'd run into the Japs. Of course in the jungle you could never see a thing except a small stretch of trail ahead. A hundred times a day you lived in anticipation through the sudden pup-pup-pup…pup-pup-pup-pup of a machine gun opening up on the column. They say, wrote General Joseph W. Stilwell, 'The coward dies a thousand deaths, the valiant dies but once.' But possibly the valiant dies a thousand deaths too, if he is cursed with imagination…. Artillery mortar and even machine gun fire could be plainly heard from less than five miles away, where the main battlefront lay. Ahead the view was always closed by a bend in the trail. Always, there was a bend to be rounded. The worst part of the campaign was, 'What was around the next bend?'"

This account reminds us that the larger fear that loomed, even for these heroic soldiers, was the constant uncertainty that loomed around the next bend. More painful than the leeches, disease, hunger, and fighting itself was the relentless uncertainty.

I never met my grandfather, but I'm fascinated by his story of courage and bravery—talk about weathering the unknown! I did some research and came across the testimony of one of the soldiers who was interviewed back in August 2018, the late Lieutenant General Sam Wilson. When asked by the journalist, "How did your time with the Marauders shape you as a soldier and as a man?" Lieutenant General Wilson replied, "I was once asked how I kept going when I was so sick. I found I had one ability—I could put one foot in front of the other; I could take the next step. And that is all that is required. One just has to take the next step. And later, when I encountered difficult situations in other times, I told myself, 'Yep, I can still take one more step.'"

On December 5th, 2019, the exact month the first Covid-19 case was discovered, and the same month I decided to start researching my grandfather's battalion, the Merrill's Marauders were finally recognized by Congress with the Gold Medal Act, awarding the last survivors of the battalion with the Congressional Gold Medal. There are only eight survivors left. Serendipitously, I asked my Uncle Billy for a personal accounting of my grandfather's time in Burma. Three weeks after receiving his accounting, at the age of ninety-two, Uncle Billy unexpectedly passed away. Uncle Billy was the last relative who could have given me a living testimony of my grandfather's experience from his memory. Based on the bizarre timing, I think the story I unearthed around my grandfather's service with the Merrill's Marauders was meant to be examined as a lesson for all of us in this post-pandemic, deeply uncertain world.

When Moses gave his final address before he died, he said, essentially, no matter what's going on, you are going to know how to weather the storm because you have weathered it—you lived through Egypt, you walked out of Egypt, you know how to do this. The only way to true personal freedom is to know deep inside your heart that you can weather the storm again. That you believe in your own capacity.

Rabbi Nachman of Breslov said, "When a person despairs, their intellect and mind go into exile." Joseph understood this intrinsically. He understood that showing up every single day with joy was the pathway to freedom, because joy is its own freedom.

When Charlton Ogden Jr. had been relieved of his duties as a Marauder, after weathering the most difficult experience of his life, he wrote in his memoir, "Happiness is what comes after unhappiness." We're in this incredible time right now. We can collect new habits, we can collect new wisdom—it's powerful and kind of exciting. Allow yourself to mourn the loss of "certainty." We have to mourn it, and we might long for it again. But when the grief finally leaves, know with deep certainty that the lessons of losing that veil will show you a different kind of magic in being alive. The unhappiness will finally lead to a happiness we have never known before. I believe life will become more wonderful in the long run. All you must do is take the next step toward dawning.

CHAPTER 18

LIGHTING THE NEW PATH

While Robbie was in the hospital, I kept thinking about my grandparents. They were in the United States military, and truly knew how to forge forward even when forward felt frightening and unpredictable.

I used to spend the second night of Hanukkah with my paternal grandmother, Bubby Shirley, before she passed away in 2019. And every year, it seemed that I managed to leave this poor woman in tears. One Hanukkah, I forgot to close the oven door when I took out the latkes; Bubbie tripped and fell, leaving her with a face bruised in a shade of blue not entirely dissimilar to those little blue candles we had just lit. The following year I was extra cautious in the kitchen and we made it through dinner, dreidel playing, and even the X-Factor without incident. Just as I figured I had cleared all the hurdles, it happened.

Bubbie Shirley handed me the matches and said, "You are the oldest. Here, you light." I lit the match and touched the blue wick that stood in the tall silver menorah. Out of the corner of my eye, I noticed a second, smaller menorah with orange candles set up. I reached to light it as well. Just as the flame hit the orange wick, my grandmother shouted, "NO! NO! NOT THAT ONE!" With fear and intimidation, I immediately blew it out, trying my best to wipe the black scar from the fragile wick.

"Chava, those candles are fifty years old! I never light that menorah! We leave that one unlit!" my grandmother cried.

Oh, the shame and guilt I felt over lighting my grandmother's antique fifty-year-old candles, which she had managed to display so flawlessly for an entire jubilee. Until me.

Bubbie Shirley was an amazing person. She weathered the storms of burying two husbands and a son, yet in spite of it all she remained incredibly steadfast in her faith. Almost every visit I had with her was spent reminiscing about my Grandpa Morton, the dashing soldier, their tremendous love affair, and the time she spent as one of the first female naval officers, and a United States Lieutenant Corporal's wife—a role she was most proud of.

As I gazed at my grandmother that Hanukkah, her eyes welling with tears, it became evident that the menorah with the orange candles I had singed had a unique and precious story. Very delicately, I asked my grandmother to share it with me.

The year was 1952, just seven short years after the Holocaust. My grandparents were stationed at an American army base in Kissingen, Germany. When the winter holiday season rolled around, the American soldiers were given the opportunity to choose from gifts that had been collected for the officers and their families. Grandpa Morton sifted through the donated items and found one lonely brass menorah among the pile of holiday toys and presents. When my grandmother saw this precious menorah, she called her cousin back home and asked her to send Hanukkah candles from the U.S. so they could light their new treasure.

The orange candles that arrived from Newburgh, N.Y., were clearly the perfect choice. My grandmother placed the orange candles in the menorah and discovered they were the perfect fit, as if the menorah was made especially for them. Brimming with Jewish pride, my grandparents lit their menorah in the window that Hanukkah. To their surprise, several German townspeople began lingering outside on their front lawn. With less than a decade separating my Jewish grandparents from the ashes of Auschwitz, fear began to creep in. Just to be safe, an officer was called to stand guard at their home as the lights burned. Men and women from all across the town came to see the lights. When asked by the officer why they were lingering in front of my grandparent's home, a German neighbor replied, "The lights, we never thought we'd see them again." Fifteen hundred Jews had been killed in this small German village. Less than seven years later, a little unassuming menorah heralded the first Hanukkah to illuminate the vast darkness the Nazis had left behind in that corner of the world.

A few short years later, the same year my Grandpa Morton died from a heart attack, the candle company that manufactured those perfectly sized orange candles went out of business. With only one last box of orange candles left in my grandmother's possession, she decided to set that menorah in the window next to the menorah that she lights each year. She kept it as a reminder of what she had lost—and of the miracle she and my grandfather witnessed together, the miracle of light in the midst of darkness.

So there were two menorahs in my grandmother's window. One tall, silver menorah that she kindled each night of Hanukkah, boasting with colors and luminous light. And a small, humble brass menorah, with fifty-year-old orange candles perfectly staged—except for the tallest one known as the "shamash," which had now been slightly singed by her granddaughter.

I do believe I was meant to light that ancient wick. For had I left it alone, this beautiful story would have never been recovered.

CHAPTER 19

SURRENDERING TO MANIFESTATION

The night before Robbie's open-heart surgery, I began thinking hard about the BEST case scenario. What did I want to ask God for? What did I want to concentrate my prayers into channeling? I told my siblings that we needed a miracle. But you can't just say "I want a miracle." You need to be intentional. You need to be specific about what you want to manifest. It's not that God doesn't know our thoughts; it's that we don't know our thoughts. So what did we think? What did we want?

I don't know why I said this, maybe it was my wishful thinking going into effect, because honestly there was not a single doctor who had indicated this could remotely be a possibility. But I told my sibs, "Guys, the miracle we have to pray on is that Robbie only needs a valve repair, not a replacement." A valve repair would mean no lifelong Coumadin. It would mean not living with the uncertainty of needing another open heart surgery down the line. According to medical journals, a repair (versus a replacement) had an excellent survival rate at 95% at 5 years and 94% at 10 years. Those were good numbers. I liked that.

"Okay," my brother Mendy said, "That's exactly what we pray on then."

"A valve repair," my other brother Yaak said. "Good. That's the miracle we'll count on."

"But guys," I said, "Don't get your hopes up, because the likelihood of that happening is awfully grim. I don't want anyone getting too attached to that outcome. But it doesn't hurt to ask."

What followed from that was a long-winded WhatsApp discussion between me and my sibs on how important it is that I stay positive. My "don't get too attached to that outcome" speech was followed by a long diatribe of "Chava, you have to believe it to be it." To which I got angry, of course, because I hate being told how to "be." And what followed that was a discourse on which birthday cake I should order for my son, Meir, whose birthday was going to fall out on the day of Robbie's surgery.

Me: Strawberry shortcake, that's the best case scenario cake.

Mendy: We need a backup plan in case they don't have that flavor.

Mimi: We are such good cake coordinators wow.

Yaak: The napoleon cake or chocolate layered cake is amazing for $4 million dollars.

Mimi: I shit $4 million dollars.

Mendy: But do they do glaze or is it the powdered bullshit that everyone does. If it's not glazed they can shove that napoleon up their asses.

Chava: If they don't have the strawberry shortcake, backup is fruit tart.

Mimi: Fruit tart? ARE YOU ON CRACK?

Yaak: Chava, he will not need a replacement, only a repair. I'm going with this version.

Mendy: I'm super optimistic now about Robbie, except for the fruit tart choice that's a terrible idea.

Yaak: Agreed.

They didn't have the strawberry shortcake so we settled on the backup: the fruit tart. And I wondered if on the day of surgery we would need to settle on the backup outcome, instead of the more ideal one I'd convinced everyone to pray for.

There was really no chance this outcome was possible. None of his doctors or surgeons believed this outcome was remotely achievable. So I channeled a little Jeffrey and Ravit Feldman "We

Got This" attitude and I surrendered to manifesting and believing in the possible. Notice I didn't say believing in the impossible. How can one believe in something that cannot possibly happen? As Jeffrey and Ravit taught me, the only way to manifest possibility is to focus on potential versus helplessness.

I have come to acknowledge that surrendering to manifestation does not mean leaving quietly or giving up. Surrendering to manifestation means you get to deliberately abdicate hopeless effort to glorious persistence on your own terms. Surrendering does not need to happen soundlessly or in a murmur, like the soft swishing sound my husband's heart made before his surgery, which threatened his life every moment for two months. For a murmur is not the sound of strength. No, it is the sound of failing. To surrender through tears and prayer does not mean we are leaning into failure. It means we are leaning into intention, ambition, preparatory aspiration.

Surrender happens with an inner violence of anger burning in our bones. Anger does not stay there forever. Anger only masks the fear of final surrender. Eventually (sometimes when forced) compliance does take over. The anger subsides and the healing surrender moves in. It is okay to allow surrender to happen with a thunderous boom of sound. It should not happen in silence. Surrendering happens while crying. Like the cries heard from the strong sound of the Shofar which prepares our souls for the reset we deserve each year. You need the reverberations to blow your body into deliverance, moving into resignation, that *yes, this is happening,* until there is a withdrawal from our own ego-driven predicted outcomes.

Surrender means relinquishing my previous terms to create new ones. It means seeing what I am supposed to learn instead of what I'd prefer to ignore. It also means revamping expectations. Neither of which I like doing.

Each year in the Hebrew month of Elul, the month before the brand new lunar year is ushered in, that is how Jewish people practice faith and finally meet God. Quietly, in our own bubbles, until eventually we come together as a community in song and prayer. As the loud booming voice of the shofar pierces through our arteries and veins, we then can collectively surrender to what is and ask God to take the burden off us as we choose new ways of coping with our difficult outcomes. We're not alone when we finally "meet" God. I mean, could you imagine meeting Him without the congregation? How intimidating that would be?

Leslie Mann was interviewed on *The Late Show with Seth Meyers* and mentioned that to get over empty nesting, she wanted to "try ayahuasca...you know, to meet God." To which Seth Meyers responded, "Why would you want to do that?" The Lord has set such high expectations, there's no way that hang out would go well without the congregation helping me through that intense performance review. Which is exactly what I imagine meeting God might look like if I was getting assessed.

God: Chava, it's great to have you here. I have a list of improvements you should probably consider.

Me: Funny, I have a few improvements *YOU* should probably consider.

So yeah, I surrendered to manifesting to that big force Leslie Mann was hoping to meet. I'm just happy I didn't have to see God's reaction when I finally did. But first, Robbie and I had to get to the actual surgery and say goodbye to one another.

AUGUST 27, 2021: DAY OF ROBBIE'S OPEN HEART SURGERY

We woke up in the morning with a feeling that it would not just be a new day, but a new life. The night before, as I fell asleep, I thought about parting from Robbie. My heart ached. Two months prior to surgery, the doctor said, "Because your heart is only working at twenty percent, you must stay calm, have no stress, don't do exercise, have no sex, eat healthy, don't have chocolate or caffeine and just don't move. You can take light walks. But only if your heart rate stays around 80."

Robbie's heart rate was 90 while he was sitting. And um, did you say NO SEX? So these new rules included, go through the biggest event of your life in physical isolation from your family because Covid might kill your already damaged heart, don't be comforted during the healing process through too much touch from one another, lest one of us should die from the excitement, (one of us being Robbie, obviously), AND both of you need to find your own corners to heal during the biggest surgery of all time. In other words, we were asked to behave like prisoners in isolation all while trying to maintain no stress. "Great," I thought. "Dude, You're a dead man." My father used to tell his patients to heal you need five key ingredients he called CHIPS! Chocolate, Hugs, Ice-cream, Prozac and Sex. Well there's a list of shit we couldn't use to get better.

On the morning of the surgery, I dropped Robbie off at the hospital at 8:30 am. We both dealt with our feelings of fear in our own corners. I was so afraid to touch Robbie. What if my soothing touch murdered him? During those months he was healing from the septic infection and awaiting surgery, Robbie distracted himself every minute with work; I distracted myself every minute with *Downton Abbey*, organizing the closet, doing lots of squats, and my all-time favorite—crying in the shower. As my Aunt Sally, who was diagnosed with Uterine cancer around the same time Robbie was sick, and who faced three months of grueling chemo and radiation, said to me, "We all deal with medical crisis differently. I can't stop watching *Sex and The City* and your uncle Steve can't stop cleaning the house."

On the morning of the surgery, I pictured our last hug, our last kiss, our last touch. I wondered if it would be our last, or just the last one before we saw each other again after his surgery. I put a lot of weight on that moment. We arrived at the hospital and sat patiently in the waiting room before the goodbyes began. He pulled out his phone, "I should probably text the family, let everyone know I made it here."

"Robbie, this is our last moment together. Can we carve this time into a sacred space without the distractions." Yes, he said. And we held each other's hands. And we breathed and we looked into each other's eyes. And we looked scared. And we said little, because the moment held the weight of our entire lives. What do you say when the world feels heavy? Not much, apparently. You just sit quietly. That's what surrender looks like. The quiet after the storm. The shock after the earthquake. The breath before the plunge. The nurse finally called Robbie's name, "Tombosky," And we kissed fast so it would not feel like the last kiss. And he said "I'll see ya later." I left the hospital, got into the car, and I took a deep breath. Because that's how you say goodbye to someone you love who is coming home. It is brief. It is not a last goodbye. It could not have been a last goodbye. Right?

I was relieved and disappointed at the same time. I was relieved we were at the end, but disappointed we had to do this isolated from one another. It was as if all the worry and fear and concern had finally melted into a place of utter serenity. Because isn't relief the first feeling you inhabit when you finally surrender and you know there's nothing left to do but allow the wave to carry you to shore? So yes. I was somewhat relieved to be at the end. This was the end of the crisis, right?

That day my brother Yaak and his son, Shalom, and wife, Dina, had arrived in New York by the graveside of our holy teacher, the Lubavitcher Rebbe. My nephew Shalom was celebrating the first time he put on Tefillin before his 13th birthday, which was in a few months. Together they would pray and ask God for a miracle for his Uncle Robbie. Tefillin is a practice whereby the head and arm connecting to the body's main artery is wrapped in leather straps while the words of "Love God with your soul and your whole heart," are uttered. The serendipity was not lost on me.

Ten days before Robbie's open-heart surgery I wrote letters. Ten letters altogether. One for each day he was scheduled to be in the hospital. I wanted him to have a piece of my heart next to his. I wondered if manifesting could heighten our chances of changing his outcome. In the tenth letter I chose to predict an outcome I decided we were entitled to. "Here's the key to manifesting," Joan Rosenberg shared with me, "You gotta write your life as if it already happened." So that's exactly what I did. I wrote Robbie's tenth letter that I knew he would read ten days after his surgery twenty days before he'd even read it, and I wrote the letter as if it already happened.

Day 10:

Dear Robbie,

To think it's been 10 days since your surgery, I am writing this letter a week before the surgery, but just writing this letter makes me feel like we are there already. I love that I can write things into being.

When I was writing my two scripts with my writing partner, Annny Minute Now *and* High On Venus, *much of what we wrote had come true in our own lives months and years later. Almost like our words had a prophecy of their own. So here's what I'm going to write now. And by the time you read this letter, it will have happened. Your surgery was successful. You did NOT need a valve replacement, ONLY a repair. You are feeling incredible on day 10. You are not in as much pain as you anticipated. You are in a wonderful head space and in a good mood.*

I hope since I've written this all down, by the time you reach day ten and you are reading this letter, we will laugh at the incredibly wise, prophetic words I have managed to write down 14 days prior.

Robbie, I know this has not been easy. But you are truly making it look easy. It's kind of crazy actually. Whenever I think, I know so much about you already, you never cease to amaze and surprise me as I watch you handle life with a positive outlook. With an ease and cleverness that is admirable. You make life full.

I love you so much. This is the last letter. But I am sure not OUR last letter. Please feel free to write me back whenever you are feeling better. Please no pressure. Take your time. There is no rush. We have apparently a great deal of time now that we have been given a second chance and I can't wait to live every second of this precious time with you.

With my deepest affection,
I love you, C

Three weeks after his surgery, Robbie finally read all ten letters.

Dear Chava,

Today is day 18 since the surgery and I have been up for hours reading all the letters you wrote for me to read while I was in the hospital. All ten letters. All thirty pages. And I cried, a lot. Mostly tears of happiness as I walked with you down the vivid memory lane you so eloquently painted in your letters through the beautiful reflections and prose. When we discovered that I would need valve replacement surgery I was devastated. I wasn't concerned about the surgery or the pain— but I was so afraid of how it might change our life. I was so excited about being able to live the next adventure of life we have been planning together, and suddenly it seemed like all of that was at risk of being drastically altered. I ultimately decided to go with the tissue valve so we could be secure in knowing we would have at least ten great years ahead to live our dreams together. When I woke up to find the surgeon was able to do a repair, I was shocked. I cried. I thanked God. Of course in reading your letter for day 10, I now know that you fully expected this little miracle and even wrote that "I would laugh about your incredibly wise, prophetic words that you managed to write down 14 days prior." How did you pull that rabbit out of your hat? I am astounded.

The cardiovascular surgeon never saw it coming. None of Robbie's images from his Angiogram or his echocardiogram ever indicated the remote possibility that his complex mitral valve was repairable. And yet, that is exactly what happened. Rather than the ninety percent blockage, he only had seventy percent blockage in his artery, which meant he would not need bypass—nor was there any indication of heart damage or endocarditis. He had made a full recovery. He stayed in the hospital for only five days and was walking several miles by day eight. As predicted in my day ten letter, Robbie's recovery was miraculous.

While Robbie's recovery would take several more months, the gift we were given was that not only would he have his health back but we were given a sense of certainty that his good health would remain for many years to come. The original bleak outcome was no longer in the cards. Today, I'm realizing that surrender is exhausting. It sort of felt like I rolled out of a massive car accident. It felt like sitting in the back seat as the car finally stops and I've checked my body and yet…. I'm not injured or bleeding—but boy, I'm shook by the entire car flip. That's sort of how a crisis feels…like I'm the ball in the soccer game and I'm waiting for the game to end so I can finally do the victory dance as I come to a complete halt.

In the words of a great sage, AKA my peloton instructor, "If you scale back, you can go stronger." If you notice your strength as you forge up that mountain, you can climb to the next summit. And if you allow surrender to happen, you can scale back and surrender to God seriously and intentionally—to the most powerful awakening we could have ever imagined. So that by the time you finally do meet God, you can wander in smiling, confident, and as hot as Leslie Mann.

CHAPTER 20

THE POCKET

An eagle soars with an elegance that, from below, looks flawlessly easy. But in reality, he is propelling his entire body with whiplash inertia as his thirty-six-inch frame carries his wingspan of six-and-a-half feet through the air. The sheer power of flexing and bending to reach for those clouds is that of a pressure washer. It might look easy, but it is actually extremely technical and takes a tremendous amount of power.

We often think that to have that sort of power, there must be a lot of pain involved. We don't like pain, so in an effort to avoid the anguish we create more distress. When we actively avoid pain, we flex more, contort harder, and spasm. We rarely glide, waltz, or spin past pain. So how does the eagle do it? How does he glide with such elegance, carrying a massive load on either side of his body and make it look, well, painless? How do we ride the wave of a crisis and make it look sexy? How do we move through this orbit of discomfort with ease?

See, in my mind, to have that sort of power—the power of an eagle—there needs to be a whole lot of internal fighting going on. It can't possibly feel effortless; it must feel immensely straining. At least, that's what I assumed before taking my first swim and voice lessons.

Both of these "sports" involve using an inner efficiency that is as nuanced as it is elegant, as powerful as it is majestic. More than anything, it requires surrendering to pain versus fighting through it. And somewhere in the margin of that surrender is where the power erupts.

There are subtleties which singers count on in their muscle memory which allows the voice to soar, much like an eagle. Likewise in swimming, there are subtleties which allow the body to glide against the rippling chain of waves which, if manipulated correctly, can help you swim even faster in a painless state. The idea that I could find this space where my body could be carried, versus me carrying my body, seemed preposterous to me. That is, until I learned how to do it.

"You're pushing too hard. You don't have to work that hard," said Stefano Langone, my voice coach (who finished 7th on American Idol—same place as Jennifer Hudson, by the way—so I knew he knew a thing or two). "You must be super Type A," my swim instructor commented. Coach Dan Halladay has worked with top

Olympic champions on a college level. "You are working really hard, and it is tiring you out," they both separately commented.

I knew these were seasoned teachers who saw the best in their students and who both knew the secret to soaring like an eagle was to find "the pocket." The pocket is the place where a surfer glides in between the power of the wave and the break of the water, where the perfect surf is found. The pocket is where the surfer finally finds his stride.

"You only have so many strokes left in this life," remarked Coach Dan, "Do you really want to push yourself so hard that you force more than you need on each lap?"

It was like the Universe was begging me to become softer. To become more still. To find the pocket you need the quiet gentleness of your soul to do the work.

See, I've had my fists up for so long, fighting through so many tough challenges and moments, that I forgot. I forgot how to go into my place of rest, my space of beauty—into the pocket. The idea that scaling back to propel myself further in any sport, let alone in life, was never something I considered. One reason I pushed hard was to avoid the pain. But in pushing *"past the pain,"* I was only creating more pain. The first thing I needed to learn was how to lean in to the discomfort. The second thing I learned upon leaning in, was that once that was achieved, there was no discomfort at all. There was only flow.

A gush of fluidity allowed my voice to hit a high F note without feeling strained. It felt effortless. I was able to swim fifty laps freestyle for thirty straight minutes without being winded once. That's a mile-and-a-half feat of straight swimming I'd never managed to successfully conquer without a whole lot of pain and suffering, until I learned how to surrender to the pocket. I didn't feel like I was in pain even once after learning how to glide, propel, and elegantly become one with the pool. That is because I wasn't fighting the pain. I was welcoming it, and in doing so, I was also avoiding it all together. Weird how that happened.

Much like an eagle, as Stefano instructed me, singing became effortless. And for the first time I realized how power works. It is not something you have to fight for. Rather, it is something you reach for. Reaching is different than conquering. Reaching takes elegance. It takes a smooth, relaxed effort. There is a softening that has to happen in the body, a loosening, an ease. And if you can soften yourself into that flow, a mightiness is unleashed that liberates you in ways you never expected.

After I burnt Bubby Shirley's orange menorah candle, her perspective on the story of her loss—that she carried for nearly fifty years—changed. That moment brought us together. It was the unexpected encore of her painful story that propelled her to the *EGBOK* stage of her life. When my grandmother stared at those no-longer-perfect orange candles, instead of noticing her painful past, she would remember the granddaughter that made it a little less perfect. She would remember her legacy as well as her loss. Her future versus her past. Her "what is" versus her "what if's." Even if that legacy lay in the hands of a klutzy granddaughter who managed to torment the hell out of her. My grandmother taught me something really precious from that experience: as a wave needs to break for the surfer to find his pocket, sometimes things get broken in our own lives in order for new light and new lessons to emerge. She became softer after that. She found herself in the pocket. I don't think you can get to the pocket without a little bit of breakage to reveal the space that holds your power.

The question we must ask ourselves when a crisis arises is this: what is the storm we might have been avoiding before our crisis got here that we are now being charged to finally face? How can we use this quiet to hear the reverberations of that pain, which we might have distracted ourselves from with work, our critical voice, or self-destructive behaviors? How can we become more aligned with our personal mission, our soul's purpose?

Being in crisis is the most opportune time to finally regain balance. It is there we are given the opportunity to become realigned in our thinking. A nurturer knows that in order to take care of others, you gotta take care of yourself first. It is a dance where the choreography is set with intention to our internal compass. We cannot ignore ourselves at the expense of helping others, but we cannot only focus on our own lives either. We have to find the balance to nurturing collaboratively.

Let's realize that we have left the comfort zone of certainty. And we are about to get stronger, more resilient, unwavering, flexible, and tenacious. Together we have become survivors. Together, we can grow more than we ever thought possible.

Some of us will be lighting that broken candle over and over to revive our spirits with a new will and a deeper understanding of how our loss has shaped us. Others will be paying attention to the blessings without having experienced significant loss yet. No matter where you are in your journey, no matter what crisis you are facing or have faced, nurture you, all of you, and realize we are only a light away from joy and revelation. And like my own father, Dr. Mike, of blessed memory, used to say, to carry us into the next moment when the going got tough, if you gently relax a little to access your flow state when the chips are down, everything will, finally, be okay.

EGBOK.

EPILOGUE

A warm glow surrounded us like a cushion of love as the cold water swam in to shore and wrapped salty drops around our bare ankles. As if the tears we had shed from a lifetime of hard miles lived were now taking new form as gentle comfort on the Pacific Ocean floor. If this was love, we could feel it embracing us on the very well-deserved vacation we were finally on together. Robbie and I, the Mexican sun, and the all-you-can-drink buffet of margaritas. It had been seven months since the initial ordeal in Las Vegas, where Robbie's life hung in the balance and my emotional state dangled right beside in some gravitational metamorphosis. It's a funny thing, almost dying, the way it forces you to grab one another with all your being and never let go. This was the only real honeymoon we ever had. There was that Jamaica trip from 2002, but we had a newborn with us and Robbie spent most of the vacation/business trip in casual meetings avoiding the shrimp bar and taking notes on the subtleties of selling annuities. We should have spent more of our time traveling together in between caring for our kids and my siblings, but we never had the time or the money. When there was anything extra, we wound up using it to give the kids family vacations. (Note to self: prioritize each other from now on.)

"Let's do something adventurous," I proposed.

"You mean like sit on the beach and people watch," Robbie threw out.

"Why is that adventurous?"

"Because it's Mexico and two people just offered me cocaine for the third time since we got here."

"Why do people think you look like someone who does blow? Is it me?"

"Chava, not everything is about you."

"Isn't it though?"

So on the second day of our honeymoon, which only took twenty-seven years to book, we found ourselves on a boat headed on an incredible snorkeling expedition. We were with ten other folks from various places around the States. There was Keisha, the Brooklyn soldier with the wicked sense of humor, traveling with her lover. There was a group of people from Tennessee that looked like their skin was burning before we even got on the boat, and the New York Puerto Rican couple Frankie and Miriam with their fourteen-year-old kid, Frankie Jr.

Frankie Senior was a typical New Yorker. Six foot two, a swagger of a well-seasoned traveler. He was proud of his years traveling the globe and his adventurous expeditions such as riding on a Jet ski from Florida to the Bahamas. A ridiculous expedition that took him four hours. It was so brave, his own wife decided to never learn how to swim. Probably just to keep Frankie Jr. from ever being an orphan. We listened intently as Frankie Senior described his many adventures, and Robbie must have sensed the bubble over my head. You know the one, where the wife looks like she's basically saying, "See honey, what's wrong with us, why don't we ever do anything adventurous??"

Clearly Frankie Senior knew his way around the ocean, which is why he eagerly jumped in first. His kid, on the other hand, seemed wary and definitely not too keen on swimming in the dark high seas. Robbie, compassionately sensing Frankie Jr.'s hesitation (and probably competitively sensing Frankie Senior's eagerness) was the second volunteer to jump into the freezing ocean with his life jacket and snorkeling gear. I was third. The last sound of humans I heard was Frankie Senior begging his teenage boy to make the jump and Frankie Jr. refusing and clutching on to his mom.

Robbie and I swam together in sync to the tune of the quiet that orbited us in this rhythmic dance. Floating on the same high note in the blue sea as the beauty engulfed us. Intertwined together, enmeshed with the sea life swimming beneath our bellies, dancing to the movement of the waves in sync, hands clasped, staring at Speckled Hinds and Blueline Tilefish and concentrating on our breath, which echoed louder in the sea than on land inside our heads. It was magical. Our mouths clasped plastic tubes, which grabbed air from the oxygen hovering above; it was uncomfortable, but we didn't mind, because the mysterious visuals we got the chance to peek into were so alluring. It captivated our hearts.

And then it happened.

You know the way the world slowly watched the evening news in March 2020 and we heard the reporter say a pandemic just hit the world, but we couldn't really fully grasp it in our brains? Yeah, that was exactly how it felt when we saw this twenty-foot bright green moray eel charging us from the depths of the ocean floor. Slinking its way toward us, we didn't know whether to watch its beauty or run from the sharp teeth gnawing their way toward us. Everything in us screamed to swim away fast, but it seemed like it was too late, because suddenly I heard Robbie say, "HE BIT ME!" My breast stroke couldn't carry me fast enough. I couldn't see because the salt clouded my eyes. In the haze of the assault I lost my flipper and all I could see was Robbie staring ahead methodically swimming away with all of his life force. We were in the ocean with a sea monster swimming after us.

You should have seen Frankie Jr.'s face staring from the boat as I yelled to Manny, the boat guide, "Manny, my husband, (yeah the one with the scar on his chest from open heart surgery) was bit by an eel!!" Robbie climbed on the boat and a murder scene unraveled as blood spurted everywhere down his leg. He was off his blood thinners by then, but his blood refused to coagulate due to a toxin produced inside the mucous of the eel's mouth called hemolytic, which destroys red blood cells, forcing your blood to stop clotting. A design flaw in my opinion. Thank you, God.

The moray eel is the largest of the eel species. Typically they live in the crevices of the ocean floor and they NEVER come to the surface. But that day, amongst fifty or more swimmers in this little patch of the Pacific, this day of all days, one massive fucker decided to take a nice chunk out of Robbie's leg just missing his tendon and main artery. Morays have teeth like corkscrews, so when they wedge into your body, they have to shred your skin to unclasp their jaw. A jaw, I might add, that opens 160 degrees. Eels are covered in slime that is highly toxic, but if their mouth touches the inside of your body, bloody hell, this is not something to take lightly. The biggest complication from a moray eel bite is infection, sepsis, and then death. Cool, cool, cool.

There was no question that if Robbie had not been swimming right next to me, that eel would have charged for me. I'm softer and the damage could have been catastrophic. To say he took one for the team would not be exaggerating. Manny, our boat guide, immediately treated the bite with anti-bacterial spray, three shots of tequila (two for me and one for Robbie), and bandaged up the wound. A nurse who happened to be on our boat suggested Robbie get looked at as soon as we get to shore and that he go on a round of antibiotics. We still finished the romantic boat ride and

Keisha even made a point to order our third round of tequilas to our new boat buddies. Suddenly we were all bound by the epic eel bite. "May we all be blessed to continuously love one another no matter what. To celebrate life, to accept one another without prejudice. And to bite the juices out of life like that eel bit Robbie's leg," toasted Keisha.

The swimming part of our honeymoon was pretty much over. That night we landed in the ER where Robbie was treated with five stitches. If you google eel bites, there are maybe fifteen reports in the entire world in the last thirty years or so, making Robbie's bite number sixteen in the last three decades. Eel bites are so rare because they never leave their habitat. Even Manny, our boat guide, who had been leading these expeditions for five years alongside Jose, his boat driver, both said they'd never seen an eel attack. The ER doctor was doubly surprised by our crazy *luck*.

As I sat in the ER next to Robbie who was concentrating deeply in his mind while being sewn up, I could feel my body sitting in the ER seven months prior. I was sweating and thinking about all the worst case scenarios. Mostly I was thinking about the fact that I needed more tequila.

That night I had a bit of a "Let's go home, the trip is ruined" moment. Robbie turned to me and said, "I know it's only two days into our seven day trip and I'm already bleeding and wounded, but I'd really like to finish this wonderful time with you." So we stayed.

There had to be a source in the Torah for eel. I began googling like a mad person, "What does it mean emotionally, spiritually, Jewishly to get attacked by an eel?" I wanted answers, I wanted this to mean something. How does this happen—what was the point OF THIS SHIT SHOW EXACTLY? And if you research enough, you can pretty much find any answer to suit the craving for reason. The Talmud references the word for eel in Hebrew as, *tzelofcha*. The root word of the word *tzelofcha* comes from the word *Tzelach*, or *Hatzlacha*, which translates as to succeed; to prosper.

And that's how I knew without a shadow of a doubt that we had finally turned a corner. When your husband who almost died seven months prior from sepsis and a heart infection gets bitten in the ass by success, you know a new dawn has finally arrived. A new dawn with less adventure, more loving, and a hell of a lot more tequila. Because, as Frankie Jr. taught us, dancing to life on land is definitely way smarter.

ACKNOWLEDGEMENTS

Having my children home all together during Robbie's several-month-long ordeal was the greatest blessing. I would not have been inspired to acquire any of life's lessons without their unconditional love and support. As much as I teach them, they continue to teach me ten-fold. Mordy, Yehudis, and Meir, this book is for you. I love the three of you with all my heart and being. Of course, a special thank you to my biggest champion of all, my wonderful husband, Rabbi Robbie, who gave me the three greatest treasures on earth and who continually loves us all so unconditionally. May you have a complete healing. I love you.

To my dear daughter Yehudis Tombosky, who's artwork made this book beautiful, I thank you! You are an incredibly inspiring artist. Keep shining your light in this ever-complicated world.

JL Woodson, you are a genius designer. Naleighna Kai, thank you for your guidance. You are both a force to be reckoned with. To Yehudis Geisinsky who never stopped calling me throughout this ordeal. You sat with me on the most difficult day of our lives, and I will forever be grateful for our 40 plus year friendship. To Nomi

Greenwald, my lifeline who told me to call a medic. You probably saved Robbie's life in that moment. Also, "I miss you," forever and always.

To my incredible siblings, this book is meant to be our living legacy. We have done some hard stuff together. All lessons worth knowing happened with you by my side and I'm grateful to have you all in my life. I love you guys more than words. To my mom for being my cheerleader, always.

Another special thank you goes to my marketing guru, who really encouraged me to write this book and who created and helped me launch my website. Viviana Cardoza, you are a light and a true friend. To Alisa Brooks, my editor, I am so grateful for your wisdom and incredible astuteness. You pushed me in those moments I wanted to give up and I thank you. To Peter Himmelman and to Karen Mckinney who provided me with much needed feedback in my most harrowing moments. You made me believe I could accomplish this big, huge, grueling beast called "A book."

Lastly, I could not have written this manuscript without the wonderful guests who took the time to speak to me on the *The Nurture Series* podcast. The experts (and incredible humans) who participated are really the ones who have made this book possible. I'm excited for you to hear the indelible wisdom that was collected over the past few months on the pod! Thank you to all my incredible guests! You are all incredibly wise and present souls, and

I've been fortunate enough to learn from each of you. I'm so grateful for your courage, your enlightened, authentic, sage advice, and your guidance on how to nourish ourselves back to greatness!

ABOUT THE AUTHOR

Chava is an award-winning filmmaker, documentarian and an expansive thought leader. As a facilitator and educator, Chava has a unique approach to crafting professional mindful meditation workshops, tailored designed training programs on discovering your personal mission and her one-on-one Masterclass she created for executives known as "The Expansive Effect." Through her profound cinematic multi-sensory approach, students learn how to tap into being present, let go of patterns which do not serve their growth mindset, and learn emotional resilience so they can channel creativity and productivity with more balance and self-awareness. Chava is a writer, host of the "Nurture Series" podcast and co-creator of "The Search" web series where she interviewed various celebrities and big thinkers asking the question, "What is the meaning of life?" Eventually, she went on tour to share her findings on the meaning of life in a multi-media presentation, which included her original music, that can be found on Soundcloud.

As a filmmaker, Chava has written, produced and directed over sixty-five short films including 2 documentaries featured in the Museum of Tolerance, a comedy pilot which won for best series in the Mediterranean Film Festival in Cannes, and a period piece, which won for best in its class at the Ashkelon Film Festival.

There is a method to Chava's madness in using so many mediums to uncover the search for truth. As Maya Angelou once wrote, "You can't use up creativity. The more you use, the more you have." Through song, the written word, and cinema, she hopes to encourage others into the land of courageous self-discovery.

A nurturer to her three children and her seven siblings, Chava is married to Rabbi Robbie Tombosky. Together they lead one of the largest west coast young professional Jewish Modern Orthodox congregations, where they give ongoing classes and workshops.

To get more information on Chava's film, articles, music and pod, head over to her website at: www.chavafloryn.com

To listen to the full interviews highlighted in this manuscript, you can head on over to *The Nurture Series* available on Spotify and iTunes.

RECOMMENDED READING

Go to my Bookshop on bookshop.org to download my recommended reading list.

(INDIVIDUAL LINKS ARE IN THE TITLES BELOW)

1. *The Seven Principles for Making Marriage Work: A Practical Guide from the Country's Foremost Relationship Expert* by John M. Gottman, Ph.d. and Nan Silver

2. *90 Seconds to a Life You Love: How to Master Your Difficult Feelings to Cultivate Lasting Confidence, Resilience, and Authenticity* by Joan I. Rosenberg

3. *The 5 Love Languages: The Secret to Love that Lasts* by Gary Chapman

4. *Getting the Love You Want: A Guide for Couples* by Harville Hendrix Ph.D., Helen LaKelly Hunt Ph.D.

5. *The Surfer and the Sage: A Guide to Survive and Ride Life's Waves* Noah Benshea (Author) Shaun Tomson (Author)

6. *The Untethered Soul: The Journey Beyond Yourself* by Michael Alan Singer

7. *Daring Greatly* by Brene Brown

8. *The Gifts of Imperfection: Let Go of Who You Think You're Supposed to Be and Embrace Who You Are* by Brené Brown

9. *Seven Core Issues in Adoption and Permanency: A Comprehensive Guide to Promoting Understanding and Healing In Adoption, Foster Care, Kinship Families and Third Party Reproduction* by Allison Davis Maxon and Sharon Roszia

10. *Let Me Out: Unlock Your Creative Mind and Bring Your Ideas to Life* By, Peter Himmelman (Amazon)

11. *You* by, Anonymous (Amazon)